Leadership Mindset 2.0

The Psychology and Neuroscience of
Reaching your Full Potential

R. Michael Anderson

Table of Contents

Introduction

The tension in the office was like a ticking time bomb. At first, I was confused when my business partner walked around my desk to where I was sitting:

"I'm going to wipe that smile off of your face," he said.

Then cocked his arm back and…hit me.

It was April Fool's Day, but this was clearly no joke.

You may be wondering what physical assault, Johnny Walker and divorce papers have to do with leadership. They're an example of what can happen when things go off the rails. They were for me, anyway.

Looking back, there was a lot I could've done to prevent the dispute with my business partner. Outwardly, the company was doing extremely well. But inwardly, I was way out of my depth, my mental state was a mess, and I was spiraling out of control.

Like me and the many leaders I've worked with—from early-stage scaleups to Fortune 500 companies like Microsoft, Uber and Salesforce—there are times when you face difficult questions that keep you up at night.

How do I handle all this responsibility? Should I even be in this role? Am I letting people down? What if I fail? Would I ever recover?

What people don't tell you is that, deep down, many leaders have a secret. Their inner voice is silently screaming at them:

You don't know what you're doing. Things are out of control. You're totally winging it and hoping nobody notices.

And that's scary as hell.

After that explosive April day, I knew I had to make major changes to my life, so I went ahead and earned a Master's degree in psychology, hired the best coaches I could find, and immersed myself in learning about leadership—as well as life. From that, I honed and implemented the tools you'll learn here in this book, and used those to turn things around.

One of the three companies I founded, Radiant Technologies, was voted the #1 place to work and landed on the Inc. 5000 list, while I was nominated for Most Admired CEO and won Social Entrepreneur of the Year.

There was another big shift: leading, which before was just one big ball of stress and self-doubt, became natural and fun. My psychology training taught me how to motivate and inspire, and it was fulfilling to see team members grow and thrive. We developed an amazing culture, so much so that word got around and industry superstars started calling us up, asking if they could work for us. One woman, a senior executive, actually camped out in front of our office, just to get a meeting with me to apply for a position. She later became our CTO.

This is the kind of success I want for you—which is why I put all the tools, skills, and habits that worked for me and the other companies I teach, into this book. Together, I call this Leadership

Mindset 2.0. It's also the basis for a new type of leadership I call Growth Leadership, which is focused on growing the leader and their team as people, while creating a high-performance culture.

Avoiding the Leadership Incompetence Trap

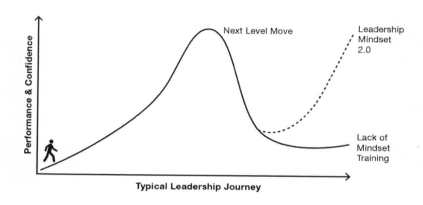

Figure 1: The Leadership Incompetence Trap

The diagram shows an unfortunate path far too many leaders find themselves on. Formerly high-performing, confident people get promoted without the proper training, support or mentoring, and find themselves in a place where they know they're falling short, and even worse, they don't know how to fix things. When this happens, not only do the leaders suffer, but so do their careers, their teams, and the company as a whole.

This was dubbed the "Peter Principle" by Laurence J. Peter in 1968, when he said "*In a Hierarchy Every Employee Tends to Rise to His Level of Incompetence.*" However, what I've found is that this is misunderstood—it's not that the employees are being put in a position they're not good at; it's that they aren't put in a position to succeed.

Think about it: the single worst action a company can take is promoting their high-performers without setting them up to succeed. Those previous superstars flounder, lose confidence, start hating their job, and either quit or—worse—stay, and become a drag on the organization.

This also happens with business owners. I run across many people—some of whom you'll read about in this book—who start a business because they have a good idea, or they are great salespeople or engineers. The business scales up, people are added, and the owner finds themselves in charge of a team that needs leadership, which they never have been trained in. The culture starts deteriorating, growth levels off, and the owner doesn't know what to do. They normally end up working more and more, in the same way they've always worked. That doesn't make a difference, so they get stressed out and frustrated, and don't know where to turn.

The good news is you can avoid this by learning and integrating the ideas in this book, represented by the dotted line in the diagram. It's designed to give you a complete roadmap for how to bypass the crashing and burning phase, and become a strategic, influential, highly-effective leader instead.

Together in these pages, we'll cover how to:

- shift your thinking and actions from tactical to strategic
- earn true respect from your team and peers
- communicate with people to facilitate their growth while empowering them, and
- develop the confidence and resilience every leader needs.

You'll also learn a lot about psychology and neuroscience, including:

- how you and the people around you are wired
- how your brain works, and how other people's brains work
- why people make the choices the way they do
- how to change your own thinking

- how to create more positive value for everyone
- ways to relate better to your team, peers both in and outside of your company, and everyone else you run across, and finally, as a bonus
- how to live a happier, better life.

Why Leadership Mindset "2.0"?

You might be wondering, *if this is Leadership Mindset 2.0, what was the first version?*

Leadership 1.0, the traditional way of leading, is top-down, "command and control" bureaucratic leadership. This just means that whoever's in charge holds the power and gives orders to whoever's underneath. The leader or boss shouldn't be questioned, and creativity, free thinking, and initiative are not encouraged. It's the way old-school militaries, monarchies, and some businesses work.

Today, research has shown that this kind leadership creates stagnation and dissatisfaction. It squashes innovation, kills profits, and destroys loyalty and trust[1]. *This is the way I was trying to lead until things almost fell apart.*

Leadership 2.0 is the opposite. It's based in the most current research we have today, and creates motivated, fiercely loyal and self-directed people with the passion to go all in. Plus, it can have a powerful impact on the bottom line, as well as on the surrounding community and society in general.

Of course, for any company culture to experience these remarkable benefits, Leadership 2.0 calls for growth from you, the leader who

---

1   Heyden, M., Koene, B., Fourne, S., & Werkman, R. (2016). *Rethinking 'Top-Down' and 'Bottom-Up' Roles of Top and Middle Managers in Organizational Change: Implications for Employee Support.* Journal of Management Studies 54(7). https://www.researchgate.net/publication/311892283_Rethinking_'Top-Down'_and_'Bottom-Up'_Roles_of_Top_and_Middle_Managers_in_Organizational_Change_Implications_for_Employee_Support

wants to go beyond old-school leadership. You do this by learning to delegate, trusting, and giving your teams what they need. Instead of authoritative control, you'll discover how to create breakthrough results through communication, vision, and teamwork. As you move into more strategic roles, you will have to keep evolving your skills, confidence, and mindset—that's how you know you're on the right track, as each level of leadership requires an updated approach.

Leadership Mindset 2.0 is a departure from decades past and a call to action: leave behind the things that we know no longer work, and make room for what does. To become a leader who jumps in and takes advantage of this new era of leadership, you will need to upskill and bring your best. This will require much more communication, and a different mindset.

CHAPTER 1:

Growth Leadership

Leadership Mindset is the key component in what I call Growth Leadership. It's called "Growth" Leadership because "growing" is the main driver of the entire system.

A leader themselves must grow in order to be successful. Once they commit to this path, they will in turn naturally coach and grow the people on their team, and as a result, their company or department will grow too, whether that be in revenue, profit, or market share. Everything a Growth Leader impacts will grow, and they will gain in influence.

Growing your team is a big part of leadership, since it's impossible to scale unless you're developing the next generation of managers to fill the need. That's what leadership legend Tom Peters meant when he said; "Great leaders do not create followers; they create more leaders."

People who commit to learning and practicing Growth Leadership will evolve personally as well as professionally, and to do so they must be self-reflective, open, and willing to change.

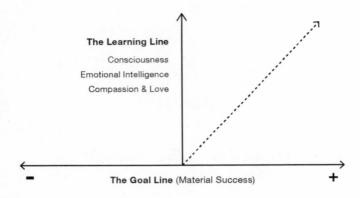

Figure 2: Growth Leadership [2]

Think of Growth Leadership as a graph with two axes (Figure 2: Growth Leadership).

There's the goal line, which is on the horizontal axis, and then there's the learning line, which goes up. The goal line is about tangible, material achievements like making more money, having a better car, etc.

The learning line on the vertical axis is about how conscious you are, how much you're learning as a person, how much you're growing and maturing, how much compassion and love you show for yourself and for others.

It's relatively easy to make progress along one of these lines. For example, it's possible to make a lot of money and never move up the learning line, never growing as a person or developing emotional intelligence. Think of the ruthless jerks who lie and play politics to "win" and get promoted.

---

2   This two-line diagram is based on a model I learned when I attended the University of Santa Monica, which I will explain more about later in this book.

You can also move up the learning line without ever being successful on the goal line. Don't we all have that one friend who is into spirituality and yoga, yet is always living on someone's couch or in a spare room, and never has any money?

The real challenge is to move along *both* axes at the same time; to keep reaching new levels of material success while also growing and evolving yourself.

What's interesting is the more money, power, and responsibility you have, i.e., the more you move forward on the goal line, the more you seem to get tested on the learning line. Often, people will stop moving on either line for one reason or another. They reach a ceiling and don't know how to bust through.

Everything I teach is designed for you to progress on BOTH axes—rapidly and consistently—at the same time.

The Growth Leadership Path

I wish I could tell you that transforming your mindset is quick and easy. It isn't. But what I *can* show you is a scientifically-developed path—based on the latest in neuroscience and psychology—that'll get you results relatively fast.

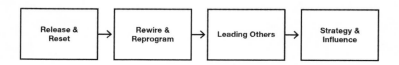

Figure 3: The Four Phases of the Growth Leadership Path

What I'm talking about is the Growth Leadership Path (Figure 3: The Four Phases of the Growth Leadership Path). This path encompasses four distinct phases, all building on each other, in order for you to create lasting, transformational change as a leader and as a person. It's not all easy. It's not all comfortable. But the payoff is huge.

As you travel along the Growth Leadership Path, you'll start to understand that your leadership boils down to your relationship to yourself. The roots of the challenges you face as a leader can be found within you. When your leadership is lacking, you'll learn how to strengthen it through your relationship to yourself. And when your relationship with yourself levels up, your leadership will too. I call this the Foundational Truth of Leadership:

> ### *Your leadership is an extension of the relationship with yourself.*

This is a core principle, and you'll get a short introduction here; you'll understand much more after getting further into the book. It means that what's happening in your outer world is a reflection of what's happening in your inner world. For example, if you find people aren't trusting you, then on some level, you're lacking trust in yourself. Or, if your team isn't inspired, there's something within you that's not inspired either.

Often when leaders come to me with issues, they want to tell me about how other people are misbehaving—what they're doing or not doing. What you'll learn here is to figure out where the misalignments are within you, and how to clean those up to create true resilience, confidence, and focus. This is how you become a powerful leader from the inside out.

When you can understand and evolve yourself, you have the makings of Leadership Mindset 2.0.

Step-by-Step Transformation

The first step to transformation is commitment. You need to be committed to the path. The reason most teams and businesses fail is simply because the person in the driver's seat never fully embraces being a leader, and they don't have the strong relationship with themselves that's needed. Instead, they emulate the people around them (who may be suffering from the same issues), deploy the "fake it 'til they make it" strategy, and keep trudging forward. This can go on for years. These half-hearted leaders try to stay invisible and avoid screwing up so badly that someone notices. After years and years of acting this way, they may have figured out how to survive, but then one morning they wake up and wonder why everything's become stagnant.

This is why there are so many stories of failure, and so many poor leaders in this world. Time after time, people focus on external survival rather than take the courageous steps to look inside, admit there's more to learn, and commit to the growth process. To take that step does take a healthy dose of strength, courage, and vulnerability—one I believe you're ready for.

Thanks to my corporate and entrepreneurial journey, and then my psychology and neuroscience education, I know exactly how to develop people like you to think like, and be, a great leader. Even if that sounds far away, and you're doubting if it's possible for you, I'm here to tell you it is. You have to be strong, you have to be open to change, and you have to have a little trust. If you have those three things, we'll get there together.

Let's get started by going through each phase of the Growth Leadership Path.

Phase One: Release and Reset

The first step on the path is one often overlooked. It's an important one—perhaps the most crucial one—when it comes to changing behavior. Just like you wouldn't pour into a glass that's already full, you have to release everything that's holding you back before you try anything new.

For leaders, this applies in two main areas.

The first thing to release, or shift, is your role and your thought patterns around it. As one of my clients says, "I need to move from being a 'doer' to a 'conductor'."

People often make it into leadership because they're good at getting things done, but now we need them to get good at having other people get things done. This is an entirely different mindset and calls for a different set of tools. After all, you've been training yourself for years to do, do, do, and it dominates your thinking. That's why, to make way for your new leadership role, you have to release your old one.

Usually, people who move into leadership are smart, work extremely hard, take responsibility for specific projects and issues, and have become excellent at a tactical job like marketing, sales, production, project management, finance, or something else. Whatever you succeeded at, you likely got very strong positive reinforcement for it, and the appreciation and praise became a motivating factor— even a subtle addiction.

But have you noticed, once you've moved into a position where you're in charge of a team, what you did before to be successful doesn't necessarily work? It used to be if a project was going off track or your team missed a quarterly target, you would roll up your sleeves and work extra hard to make things a success. It doesn't work like that now. That's called micromanaging and playing into your superhero image. Keep doing that and you'll burn out, and your team won't grow or take responsibility.

This is also the perfect example of why the first step in growing your leadership is to release your old role, and the behaviors that came with it.

To support you in this, you'll get a chance to get specific feedback on exactly where you are at as a leader in the Leadership Mindset Scorecard, right after this chapter.

In addition to your 'doing' role, there's a second important thing to release in phase one of the Growth Leadership Path, and that's the beliefs and past conditioning that are keeping you stuck. Many of the most successful leaders I work with start out by saying "I know I have blindspots. I want you to help me find them and overcome them." That's what we're going to do here.

The first step in overcoming your blindspots is releasing your outdated beliefs. Beliefs are simply any idea you hold as true. These can be certainties or possibilities, like "I'm not worthy of this success", "People never respect me", or "I'm not a natural leader." We all have beliefs that come from different sources: how we were brought up, what we learned from whoever raised us, what we didn't learn based on our life experience; even the political or economic climate we live in can create beliefs that become our reality.

What many people don't realize is that many of our beliefs are subconscious, so we don't even know we're impacted by them. Also, beliefs are a choice. We can choose new ones anytime, which we'll look more at later as well—specifically, the beliefs that limit you as a leader.

Releasing a subconscious self-limiting belief is the single most powerful shift you can make. That's why the Growth Leadership Path starts here. By getting rid of what's no longer effective, you clear the path to rewiring and reprogramming yourself.

Phase Two: Rewire and Reprogram

In Phase One of the Growth Leadership Path, we look at your role, your self-limiting beliefs and we clear the crap (that's the technical term.) With a clean slate, we can shift to rewiring and reprogramming your leadership mindset from the ground up.

I don't throw the word 'transformation' around a lot, but after getting punched by my former business partner in the middle of the day, and then devoting the next decade to my professional and personal growth, I can honestly say my leadership transformed. People ask "What is it that you learned? How did you make such a dramatic change?"

That's easy to answer. I used to be the guy who made a lot of money and wanted to show off how cool he was, but it was all coming from an insecure place. I could be argumentative, opinionated (not in a good way) and frankly wasn't very likeable. Those were the things that mattered to me; they were my old beliefs, that money and status gave me some kind of worthiness and importance.

I was under a massive amount of pressure, most of it self-created, once again because of the beliefs I held as true. I felt as if I had to control the world while looking and acting a certain way. Only after a lot of pain did I realize I needed to recreate the person I was trying to be. Rewiring and reprogramming created my new life. Essentially, I transformed my relationship with myself—and when I learned to know, like, and trust myself, everything changed.

As we help you rewire and reprogram, we get to have some fun while rebuilding your relationship with yourself. You'll discover new beliefs and explore innovative thought patterns, and the result will be unshakable confidence and self-esteem rooted in humbleness, compassion, and empathy. This will enable you to overcome any imposter syndrome, self-doubt, or critical self-talk that has caused you issues in your past. It will support you as a powerful, authentic, resilient leader that people respect.

While all of this is designed to address you as a leader, as we move to Phase Three we'll shift the focus to who you lead.

Phase Three: Leading Others

Based on your new sense of self, we can shift our attention to how you relate to, and lead, others. Here, you'll learn how to motivate, inspire, and engage people; create an amazing team culture; make difficult decisions; delegate; and even ways to hold people accountable.

Something that often isn't talked about is the immense amount of pressure leaders find themselves under. It's so all-encompassing that many people don't even notice it anymore, but as this pressure gets studied further, we're discovering it leads to health issues including burnout, sickness, and substance abuse.

When you implement the Growth Leadership System step-by-step, you'll find that you have much less stress. You'll understand your role as the leader much better, you'll empower and manage your team to be more efficient and effective, and, most of all, you'll have confidence that you can handle whatever life decides to throw at you. The self-sabotage and negative self-talk will go away; your new inner programming and wiring will lead you to bring out the best in others.

The best part is you'll learn how to do all of this while helping your team grow as people, which most leaders find the most fulfilling part of the job. If you're someone who micromanages or tries to control outcomes with your teams right now, you're in for a treat—you're going to get to witness people flourish both as colleagues and human beings. As they become empowered and take on more responsibility, you'll realize your team is starting to lead itself.

Phase Four: Strategy and Influence

The final phase in the Growth Leadership Path is about going beyond tactical success, and becoming a strategic and influential leader.

At this point, you've done a lot of releasing, you've rewired a good part of your thinking, and you know how to inspire others. You're well on your way to embodying a new leadership mindset and the final step is to help you "become strategic."

Becoming strategic isn't anything I've seen taught before, and that's why it's so exciting to bring you this phase. It's not about *having a strategy*—that's relatively easy. Many times a strategy is developed once a year, or handed down from corporate. This is about learning how to *think*, *act*, and *relate* strategically, so that you not only make it to the senior leadership team or scale your business, but also fit in once you get there.

You'll learn how to talk to a CEO, CFO, chairperson, board member, or investor—and, just as importantly, have them see you as a strategic player. You'll be the person they ask to lead the most crucial initiatives and attend important meetings. You'll learn how to carry yourself in those situations, not just by participating here and there, but instead by confidently joining in the strategic discussion. You'll also gain the respect of other people in these meetings by how you engage.

In other words, in this final phase, get ready to experience your full power as a leader. Let's face it, leadership can be difficult. It often is not intuitive. But above all, it's a game of mindset, and a game you can win.

What I want most for you and leaders like you is to be able to look back at your career and your life with pride, because you made the decision to live up to your full potential and do the most with what you were given. If you do that following the practical guidance in the pages to come, I have no doubt the world will be a better place. That's the ripple effect of a highly effective leader utilizing Growth Leadership.

Where you're headed, you'll be called upon to blaze new paths. You'll be asked to help people grow, to delight customers, and to create a real lasting impact in the world. Whether that happens or not comes down to how much courage you have to look inside of yourself and be honest about what you find or don't find, and your willingness to change. Your experience in the years ahead depends on your commitment to evolving yourself, and the four phases in the Growth Leadership System are designed to support that.

This book will teach you the fundamentals of neuroscience, psychology, and learning, and then walk you through each step of the path. But before we get into all that, here's a short, interactive assessment for you to run through to get a clear picture of your current leadership effectiveness.

CHAPTER 2:

The Leadership Mindset Scorecard

More and more, research in behavior and brain science is showing us that it's possible to apply scientific and psychological principles to leadership. Take a moment now to fill in the Leadership Mindset Scorecard below. It will help you measure where your mindset is now, giving you data to support your journey through the rest of the book.

You can fill it out the old-fashioned way using a pen, you can download the PDF at RMichaelAnderson.com/ScorecardDownload

or you can fill it in online at RMichaelAnderson.com/Leadership-Scorecard (QR code below):

If you do it online, you'll receive a report with additional information tailored to your results.

As you go through the questions, be as honest as you can, keeping in mind that you have to identify your blindspots to address them. Often, just the act of going through the questions will give you insights into your current effectiveness as a leader. Move quickly through the questions, and when in doubt, go with the first answer that comes to mind.

For each question, give yourself a 1 to 10 rating. For example, if you're in the middle, you would give yourself a "5".

PEOPLE'S PERCEPTION OF YOU

Strategic – External		My Score (out of 10)
People see you as a tactical manager; no one asks your opinion	= 1	
The other leaders see you as a critical strategic player; people come to you for strategy/strategic thinking	= 10	

Team Respect		My Score (out of 10)
Your team sees you as a boss or manager	= 1	
Your team sees you as a leader	= 10	

Strategic Network		My Score (out of 10)
You don't have many trusted relationships with people your level or higher	= 1	
You are close, formally and informally, with the major power players	= 10	

Influence		My Score (out of 10)
You don't participate in high-level meetings; or when you do, it's not effective	= 1	
You are very involved in important meetings, giving productive input all the time	= 10	

PEOPLE'S PERCEPTION OF YOU	Total Score (out of 40)	

STRATEGIC MINDSET

Decision Making		My Score (out of 10)
You feel you just make random decisions with no strategy	= 1	
You feel that every decision you make is guided by a strategy	= 10	

Time Management & Prioritization		My Score (out of 10)
You never have time / get to do the important, strategic work you want to get done	= 1	
You prioritize strategic projects and achieve them on time	= 10	

Delegation		My Score (out of 10)
You have way too many tasks assigned to you	= 1	
You hand off everything except for necessary management and leadership tasks	= 10	

Strategic Thinking		My Score (out of 10)
You never take time to reflect and think strategically	= 1	
You block out time in my day / week to think strategically	= 10	

STRATEGIC MINDSET	Total Score (out of 40)	

STRATEGIC LEADERSHIP

Career / Business (if owner)		My Score (out of 10)
Your career / business seems to have stalled	= 1	
Your career / business has been growing quickly and consistently	= 10	

Career / Business Future		My Score (out of 10)
You have no idea where your career / business will go	= 1	
You can see the next few steps of your career clearly / You can see how your business will grow very clearly	= 10	

Purpose / Mission / Values / Vision		My Score (out of 10)
No one knows, or cares, about the purpose / mission / values / vision	= 1	
Everyone knows and is bought into the purpose / mission / values / vision and it is talked about regularly	= 10	

Your Passion		My Score (out of 10)
You don't enjoy your work and it seems like a drag	= 1	
You love what you do and can't wait to get into work every day	= 10	

STRATEGIC LEADERSHIP	Total Score (out of 40)	

YOUR INNER WORLD

Stress		My Score (out of 10)
Your stress levels are affecting your sleep, moods, eating, health or relationships	= 1	
You have a healthy amount of stress and manage it well	= 10	

Self-Esteem		My Score (out of 10)
You feel like you don't belong, you are a fraud, often doubt yourself	= 1	
You know have the ability to be a leader and relish the challenge	= 10	

Confidence		My Score (out of 10)
You doubt yourself and feel like you're just winging it	= 1	
You know that whatever happens, you'll figure it out	= 10	

Conflict		My Score (out of 10)
You avoid conflict, or you lose your temper	= 1	
When there's a difficult conversation to be had, you calmly address it with a well thought out approach	= 10	

YOUR INNER WORLD	Total Score (out of 40)	

TEAM LEADERSHIP

Engagement		My Score (out of 10)
Your team seems like they are going through the motions	= 1	
Everyone is highly motivated and focused, and people take pride in the success of the team and company	= 10	

Team Attitude		My Score (out of 10)
People are generally negative, critical and gossip	= 1	
There's a sense of excitement around and people are very positive	= 10	

Openness		My Score (out of 10)
Your meetings are boring, and no one brings anything new or exciting to the table	= 1	
Your team can respectfully disagree, even with you, and is creative while taking risks	= 10	

Commitment		My Score (out of 10)
Meetings can start late, deadlines are missed often	∞ 1	
Meetings start on time every time, people hold themselves and others accountable	= 10	

TEAM LEADERSHIP	Total Score (out of 40)	

PEOPLE'S PERCEPTION OF YOU	
STRATEGIC MINDSET	
STRATEGIC LEADERSHIP	
YOUR INNER WORLD	
TEAM LEADERSHIP	
GRAND TOTAL (out of 200)	

Once you've answered these questions and tallied up your result, you'll have a clear idea of the areas to focus on.

CHAPTER 3:

Learning Like a Leader

As you go through the chapters ahead, you may look back at different times in your life with an inner voice that says,

Wow, was I ever ignorant back then. Why didn't I do things differently and save myself a ton of headaches?" Or, *"Wow I've had these beliefs for so long, ever since I can remember. I must be really screwed up!*

It's important that you NOT get caught up in the past. Every single person in the world can point to things they could have known before. But this type of self-judgment and negative analysis will only hold you back. Instead, keep in mind that in the past you've been successful. And what you're learning here in this book will make you even more successful and accelerate your career, your leadership, and you as a person.

In fact, think of reading and applying what you learn here as your **natural evolution** into a strategic, confident, highly effective leader, because the word "evolution" honors what you've done already. That's why this is Growth Leadership—you're leveling up and that's exciting.

The Three Levels of Learning

Recently on a yoga retreat, I met a senior leader at the BBC. She was a powerful, experienced executive, in charge of a big team at one of the largest, most prestigious companies in the UK, and a tier 1 global brand. When I told her about this book, which I was writing at the time, she replied:

"I love things like that because I know I have blindspots. I may know a lot of the things, but I forget some, or there's areas I need to bump up. Please do let me know when it's out. I'm sure it will also help me coach others on my team."

The fact that she was so focused on learning and improving herself, without ego, brought home how the best leaders take any situation and see how they can use it for their advancement.

Whenever you're exposed to a concept, whether it's new or something you know already, you can take one of three approaches.

Level 1: Focus on Others

Let's say you learn how the brain is wired, which we cover in a chapter coming up soon. In Level 1 learning, you take in the content and it occurs to you,

Hey, Bob in Sales could really use this! He's uptight and gets angry easily. Understanding some neuroscience would be a huge benefit to him.

This surface level learning is something that people do to appease their ego. Even though they have the opportunity to grow, they're focused on someone else instead of themselves.

Level 2: Reflect on the Past

In this second level of learning, you're going deeper. You connect to how you're already using this information, or where you've used it in the past.

I remember that conflict management article I read last year. It seemed to work pretty well when I had to fire that Ops guy.

While this level of learning is aimed at you instead of others, it is still justifying something you've done already (or are already doing.) Growth is limited at best.

Level 3: Committed to Growth

Level 3 Learning is where the gold is. It's when you take a good, hard look at yourself and find out where you aren't applying something as deeply as you could. Then, you make a plan to change that. Leaders understand that level 3 learning is actually easier when you learn something brand new. However, how often are you exposed to something you've heard before, and think o*h yes, I know that,* and then forget all about it?

Where real courage and character come in is when you hear a concept again, and think, *where can I do this better? How else can I apply and integrate this?*

It takes work to be a high-performing leader, and it also takes the resilience to continually reflect on your state and actions to see how you can improve. The reason this takes resilience is by doing so you have to admit you still have something to learn, and your ego doesn't like that. Speaking of ego, let's learn more about that now.

Exploration

To support you to integrate what you're learning in your everyday life, you'll find some self-reflective prompts throughout the book. Take some time to engage with them to get the highest return on your reading investment.

What is your mindset right now as you read this book? Are you looking to validate what you already know, or are you ready to honestly reflect on your life and see how you can evolve and grow?

> Think about the last time someone gave you feedback. Were you defensive? Or did you search everywhere in your life for where you could apply the feedback at a deeper level?

One more note about learning: I have a free community which has additional trainings, downloadable tools, and more. You can join through Facebook: RMichaelAnderson.com/FBGroup

and LinkedIn: RMichaelAnderson.com/LIGroup

Two Parts of a Leader's Consciousness

There are two parts to any human's consciousness. The first part is your natural state—what we call the authentic self. When we're in our natural state, we're connected. We're at peace. Things are aligned and feel good.

The second part of your consciousness is your ego, which is designed for one simple thing: *to protect you.* When your mind or body perceives a threat, it moves you out of your natural state—the authentic self—and has the ego take over. The ego addresses the perceived threat by creating comfort, control, and security in whatever way it can, using whatever's available. The ego isn't necessarily bad, it's just overused. In fact, the ego's defenses have served humans well for 20,000 years, especially when we needed constant protection. Until just a few generations ago, we were often fending off or hunting wild animals, or at war, fighting neighboring nations to survive.

The Stress Response System

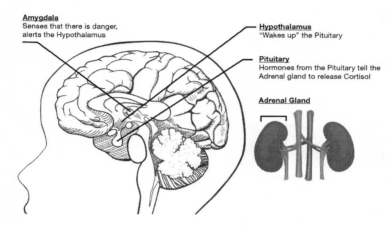

Figure 4: Your Stress Response System

What happens in your brain in the presence of a threat (Figure 4) is that your stress response system kicks in. This begins with the hypothalamus–pituitary–adrenal axis (knows as the HPA axis.) When the almond-sized brain structure called the amygdala senses there's danger, it tells the hypothalamus, which wakes up the pituitary gland. The pituitary gland then releases hormones, which travel to the adrenal glands on top of the kidneys, which in turn release cortisol. This process is what tells the rest of the body to be on guard.

All this happens in a split second—less time than it took you to read that paragraph—and that's what happens when you shift into your protective ego state.

Luckily, the hunt for food now consists of getting Deliveroo or opening the fridge, and the chances of dying from an arrow or spear are next to nil. The issue is that we've been wired for the ego to protect us in a certain way for the last, say, 19,800 years, and we haven't rewired ourselves to adapt to modern society. Our brain doesn't recognize—until we teach it to—that there's no longer a need to protect ourselves the way it used to.

Instead of physical danger, today you're exposed to constant low-level stress that can provoke the shift into your ego. Think about how it's trying to protect you when you attend a critical board meeting. Or, when you're afraid someone is vying for your job. Or even when someone clearly isn't performing in their role, but you're resisting having that difficult conversation.

In each case, your ego thinks it's being called into service as your protector, even though it's interfering at the exact wrong time, causing you to behave in an unhelpful way. After all, what do you think imposter syndrome is? It's your ego thinking it needs to protect you from a situation it's not comfortable with. (More on imposter syndrome later…)

How else are ego and your authentic self—the two parts of a leader's consciousness—relevant to your leadership? Simply put, all poor leadership behaviors and habits are ego-driven. When leaders micromanage and try to control everything, that's all ego-based behavior rooted in an instinct to protect. The same applies when managers blame people, don't take responsibility, or hide things.

Whenever we get stressed, whenever we get angry, even when somebody comes to us with harsh energy, we react in the same way neurologically—as if we're being physically attacked. You might start feeling hot, tense, even tight or tingly in your neck, chest, or somewhere else. These are the physical symptoms that come up when the ego kicks in and gets defensive. Your brain and your body are ready for battle, even if it's only one within an office.

Figure 5: The Ego & the Authentic Self

As you can see from Figure 5, our egos and authentic selves are opposite each other. You can never be in the ego and the authentic self at the same time. You can be MORE in your ego, or MORE in your authentic self, but never both in a given moment. We need to get you out of the ego into your authentic self, because that's the state that powerful leaders operate from.

Think about the traits of great leadership. Things like trust, teamwork, empowering others, or sharing the credit...see how those come from people who are in their authentic self, and don't feel the need to protect themselves?

By shifting into your authentic self, into a place of peace and calm, you'll have much more self-esteem , you'll be more likable, people will trust you more, and you'll connect with people much more easily [3][4][5]. That all comes as a result of trusting ourselves and em-

3   Iqbal, S., Farid, T., Khan, M. K., Zhang, Q., Khattak, A., & Ma, J. (2019). *Bridging the gap between authentic leadership and employees communal relationships through trust.* International journal of environmental research and public health. https://www.ncbi.nlm.nih.gov/pmc/articles/PMC6982109/

4   Whitehouse, J., Milward, S., Parker, M., Kavanagh, E., & Waller, B. (2022). *Signal value of stress behaviour.* Evolution and Human Behavior. https://www.sciencedirect.com/science/article/pii/S1090513822000162

5   Wood, A., Linley, P., Maltby, J., & Baliousis, M. (2008). *The Authentic Personality: A Theoretical and Empirical Conceptualization and the Development of the Authenticity Scale.* Journal of Counseling Psychology 55(3). https://www.researchgate.net/publication/42739517_The_Authentic_Personality_A_Theoretical_and_Empirical_Conceptualization_and_the_Development_of_the_Authenticity_Scale

powering others. Working from your authentic self will turn you into a long-term successful leader—and help you a heck of a lot on the personal front as well.

It's also the state you need to be in to be creative and think strategically. Many people tell me they get inspired ideas in the shower. There's a reason for that. Showers are typically protected spaces where the ego can relax and lower its guard. The door's locked. Nobody can bother you. It's warm. The ego lets go of its hold on you, then you relax into your authentic self and your best ideas come through. You're going to learn how to cultivate and make this relaxed, open state more natural for you, so you can experience it through the day, not just in the shower.

As you're introduced to these concepts, think of them as the foundation of a building. Everything you learn here will support what you learn later. Many people get huge insights from learning and applying these foundations as they apply in almost every situation. For example, when I sent a note to the BBC executive I mentioned earlier, to get her permission to include the anecdote in the book, she replied, "Sure, I even still have a post-it note in front of my zoom screen that says 'authentic self not ego self,' so your teachings have impact!"

Exploration

When do you shift into your ego? Is it around a certain person, or certain type of people? Is it in a certain place or context (e.g. meetings, in front of a large group, when you meet new people)?

What are the physical signs that you're in your ego? Do things speed up? Do you feel tightness anywhere (e.g. chest, neck, head)?

How do your thoughts, behaviors, and actions change when you're in your ego?

Becoming aware of when you're in your ego in real time is often enough to shift you right back into a neutral state of mind, if not all the way into your authentic self.

The ARC Process

The next way to learn like a leader involves a three-step process called ARC, which stands for Awareness, Response, and Compassion.

ARC: Awareness

Einstein once said, "If I had an hour to figure out the most important question in the universe, I would spend the first 55 minutes making sure I understood the question." That's what awareness means. It's about slowing down and getting to the heart of the real issue.

Early on in my leadership, I was always go-go-go, running at a thousand miles per hour. I would tell you that I COULDN'T slow down because I had too much to do. But sprinting like that all the time doesn't work. You end up fixing symptoms, you aren't strategic, and are always trying to play catch-up. My ADHD would make me reactionary—things would come up and I would jump on them. This created a lot of extra work and caused issues in relationships with employees, customers, and partners.

In the Awareness stage of the ARC process, you slow down and ask yourself, *"What's the real issue? What am I trying to solve here?"* Because what we think is the problem initially often isn't what's actually wrong. I'll give a few examples in the next step.

ARC: Response

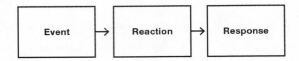

Figure 6: Reacting vs. Responding

If reacting and responding sound similar to you, that's because they are, but there's a subtle yet meaningful difference (Figure 6). A *reaction* is immediate and often emotionally charged. It's what your leg does without you even trying when the doctor taps your knee—a knee-jerk reaction. Whereas a *response* is thought out, intentional, and strategic. It would be like moving your leg in a thoughtful way in order to kick a ball into the net. You're choosing that movement.

A reaction is immediate, automatic, and often emotional. If left unchecked, the reaction will continue to drive your behavior. A response is measured, strategic, and thought through. It can interrupt or override the reaction.

Reacting isn't necessarily *bad*. It's just that our initial instincts aren't always optimal for the situation. Instead, simply pausing in order to move from reaction mode into response mode can make all the difference between a successful and an unsuccessful outcome.

Here are two examples:

If someone is 10 minutes late for a meeting, your reaction may be that you're frustrated and even angry. Using the ARC process, you slow down and have an awareness that you need to find out why they were late. Your response is to call them and ask calmly why they're not there. They explain that they were in a small car accident and had to deal with that.

You're in the middle of a board meeting and the president asks you a detailed, technical question you weren't prepared for. Your (egoic) response is to defend yourself, but you take a second to compose yourself, have the awareness that this question came out of the blue, and calmly respond that you weren't prepared for this question. Then the president realizes she asked the wrong person and redirects her inquiry.

In these quick yet common examples, the situation could become problematic if the initial reaction were allowed to take over instead of pausing for awareness, and choosing a strong response.

AR<u>C</u>: Compassion

I don't know about you, but no one can ever be as hard on me as I am on myself. The high performers I know get so used to striving for perfection, focusing on what went wrong, and picking out mistakes that they train themselves to always look for the negative and get stuck there. All that stress plus responsibility is a formula for trouble—and that includes burnout and even depression. That's why compassion is crucial—for other people, including our teams, but mainly for ourselves.

Remember, your leadership is a reflection of the relationship with yourself. That's why we focus on ourselves first. Self-compassion means giving yourself a break when you're not perfect.

Much of what you'll learn in Growth Leadership will change that negative voice in your head so that it stops being so critical. Not only will you silence the negativity, but you'll ultimately move all the way to being your own biggest supporter. After all, where do you think successful risk-taking, confidence, and resilience come from? A strong sense of self-compassion.

Let's look at a more detailed example that runs through the ARC process.

Imagine that the performance of one of your team members has dropped off the last few weeks and your largest client just called you directly to complain. What's worse, they intend to terminate their contract with you. You're the leader and it's up to you to address this. What do you do? Let's apply the ARC process:

Step 1: Awareness

Contrary to what you're used to doing, which is likely to jump into action, the growth available to most leaders is to take a moment to pause and get curious. When you do that, you'll find that a bunch of questions come up. Such as:

What's going on with your employee? When did you start noticing their change in behavior? Has something changed in their personal life? What else do you know could be affecting them—after all, they've been a good employee for years, so why has their behavior changed now?

Don't forget to also ask what's going on with YOU around this. As their leader, are you angry at them? Frustrated?

That's the first part of this process.

Step 2: Response

Given the nature of the complaint from a very important client, it's natural for you to be angry or frustrated. But will being angry or frustrated help solve this issue? Of course not. Taking a step back, being strategic and smart, what measured response can you choose instead of reacting off-the-cuff?

Even though you don't like conflict, certainly you could talk to the team member. You could also hop on a call with the CEO of the client company to see if you can win them back. If you can't, you can at least ask for feedback to get insight on what to change for next time.

You could also call a company meeting and find out how to put in systems so you never lose a customer like this again. You might find a way to empower the sales team to achieve this. If we all did that every time we lost a client, would we be a better company at the end of the day? Of course we would.

All of these are examples of thoughtful responses instead of re-actions. For the sake of this example, let's pick one—talking to the employee—and finish applying the ARC process. How do you handle going to the employee to talk about the lost client?

Start by remembering the two parts of your consciousness—your ego and your authentic self. This is a great moment to ask, "Are you in your ego or your authentic self?" If you're angry, frustrated, anxious, or all three, then you're in your ego. It's trying to protect yourself, and throwing up those emotions as a shield.

How would being in your authentic self look in this case? If you remind yourself there's no tiger chasing you, and shift your protec-tive ego to one side, does the idea of a conversation become easier? Choosing a response rather than reacting from your ego is the sec-ond step in the ARC process.

Step 3: Compassion

Finally, after pausing to become <u>A</u>ware, then choosing a <u>R</u>esponse rather than a reaction, the last step in the ARC process is to apply <u>C</u>ompassion. Because you've slowed things down, you're able to see the bigger picture beyond the urgency of the lost client. This allows you to have empathy for your employee, as well as the client and the company bottom line.

When you enter a conversation with someone and you are in your ego, they will sense this and get in their ego. When people are defending themselves, their only goal is to get out of the situation as quickly and as safely as possible. Learning and growing are practically impossible. When you enter into the meeting and you're in your authentic self, they will do the same, and be open to a productive conversation.

Approaching your employee with compassion may sound something like this:

"Hey, I just got a call from XYZ customer. They let me know you haven't delivered their services and want to terminate. Is everything all right? You're normally great with this client."

Since you've worked on your presence through the above steps, your employee can feel your empathy. They know you're there to support rather than attack them, and the conversation goes smoothly.

In my experience, approaching things with compassion and curiosity is extremely effective. It shows you're looking to solve the issue—almost like a detective—and are coming in with partnership energy instead of blame. Blaming or reactive energy will only make the employee feel they need to protect themselves—that'll put them in their ego and any collaboration will go out the window.

Walking through the scenario of the lost client highlights the way the ARC process—Awareness, Response, Compassion—naturally elicits empathy, emotional intelligence, vulnerability and authenticity from you as the leader, as well as from your team.

As a leader, you always want to create a situation with the best chance for getting a positive result. This is a simple way to do just that.

Exploration

Think of a situation that didn't go very well over the last few days. Now, run that through the ARC process and see how you could have handled that differently.

Awareness: What was the real issue?

Response: You probably reacted. What's a different response you could have chosen?

Compassion: Did you get down on yourself and/or someone else?

Now, think of an upcoming situation that may happen over the next few days. How can you proactively apply the ARC process to that so you can create a more favorable outcome?

The Illusion of Control

The concept of control is an important one in psychology. To understand this better, here's a question for you: Do you think a salesperson can control whether they hit their quota in a month or a quarter? Think about it for a second.

The answer is no, actually they can't.

There's a lot they can do to *influence* their sales success: make cold calls, learn about the product or service, get a coach, or listen to their manager. But they can't control the actual outcome. Let me tell you how I know this.

I was a salesperson for an enterprise software company during the 9/11 terrorist attacks. Not one salesperson in our company hit their quota during that time. There was nothing any of us could do to make more sales. The market ground to a halt. While not every scenario is that extreme, it illustrates that some circumstances are out of our control.

(It also doesn't mean we should keep salespeople who consistently miss their quota, though it does mean we should focus on things that they can control.)

Now let me ask you another question. Salesperson aside, what is the only thing you can control?

If you said yourself, you got it. We can control our thoughts (at least some of them), our beliefs (again, some of them), and pretty much all of our actions. That's it. NOTHING ELSE IS IN YOUR CONTROL.

We can't control our bosses, teams, colleagues, customers, partners, or even our kids. Wouldn't it be great if we could? I bet you've tried a few times as well, eh? Joking aside, when I learned this truth about control, it changed how I viewed the world, and it can for you, too.

One of the things you can control is your response to things. So, the goal is for you to become mindful and strategic about how you do that. Ideally, your responses take into consideration what's best for your team, for your company, and for the overall situation.

One of my teachers called control the ultimate addiction. I can see why. It's hard to let go of control completely, and in reality, you shouldn't. You're a manager and a leader—you're there to be in control of some things. Just not everything.

Stress is what arises when we're trying to control something that we can't. *Am I going to land this deal? Is this employee going to quit?* Acknowledging that we can't control what happens and instead focusing on what we *can* control is incredibly freeing.

In fact, that's a great life hack; anytime you're experiencing stress, think about what you're trying to control that's actually out of your control. Reflecting on this is often a way to come into a more calm and peaceful mindset. At the end of the day, you'll be much more successful when you learn to let go of control of the right things. Your energy will be on the things that move the needle... not the needle itself.

Are you (via your ego) controlling a situation because of fear? Or are you trying to control it to help others? Consider your deeper motivation. When you're being respectful of everyone's time and energy, that's operating from your authentic self rather than seeking to seize control.

Exploration

Where do you often go overboard with control?

Where are you experiencing stress? What are you trying to control that's out of your control?

What *can* you control, to influence the outcomes you have in mind?

A Practical Approach to Mindfulness

You know that feeling when everything seems to be going a hundred miles an hour and you're hanging on for dear life? Or when you're so overwhelmed that no matter how much you do, you feel it doesn't even make a dent in your to-do list? Or when you talk to a high-level person and they lay out a strategic plan that should've been obvious but you never saw it in the first place?

On the other hand, have you ever come back from a relaxing vacation with your mind so clear and relaxed that you can remember every detail, operate with a clear head, and feel connected to everything going on around you? As various studies[6] have shown, that's what mindfulness brings you.

Personally, once I started developing my mindfulness, I found that I had much more patience, I could connect to other people much more easily, I let go of a lot of stress, and I could see patterns and strategy effortlessly. That's why it's key for leaders, and why I

---

6   Staff, M. (2022, August 31). The science of mindfulness. Mindful. https://www.mindful.org/the-science-of-mindfulness/

initiate 3-minute meditations at the beginning of many trainings and board meetings. (I call them centerings, as some people have misconceptions about meditations.)

To become mindful is to become more in touch with the world. You can see how everything fits together. Life slows down and you become part of its flow. From this state it's far easier to tap into your intuition and your authentic self. Mindfulness is achieved through stillness and quiet and the main tool for achieving more mindfulness is meditation.

Meditation

Speaking of meditation, the easiest way to get started is with an app like Insight Timer or Calm, through a guided meditation, although I encourage you to also give silent meditation a try. When your thoughts start to wander, don't worry. I've been practicing seriously for over a decade and thoughts still pop into my mind frequently when I'm meditating.

Because many people find it difficult, here's a simple way to get started:

- The ideal time to meditate is just after waking up and using the bathroom, before the rest of your house wakes up. (This has to do with the state of your brain.) If that's not possible, do your best to fit it in wherever you can, as long as it's not on a full stomach.
- Find a quiet, peaceful place, ideally not the same place you work, watch TV, or do another activity. (Your brain links the place you are at with the activity you are used to.)
- Sit on a chair where you're comfortable and your back is as straight as possible.
- Set a timer for however long you want to meditate. You could start with two minutes and work up to five or more.

- As you start the timer, sit up straight with your eyes closed. Gently breathe natural breaths and concentrate on feeling the breath come in and out of your nose.
- When a thought comes into your mind—and thoughts WILL come into your mind—gently smile and let it flow through your mind, then return to your breath.

That's it, you just meditated.

Especially if you have a hard time focusing—say you're fidgety, distracted, or get confused like many of the clients I work with— you'll want to give this some effort. My own ADHD used to be so severe, I felt like a caged animal. I couldn't concentrate for more than a few seconds, my mind would constantly chatter, and I wouldn't even make eye contact with people.

Now, the world has slowed down so much for me—giving me more time and space to make intelligent, proactive, and creative decisions. Before I felt out of sync with the world; now I feel in the flow. People often tell me I have a very calming presence, which is the opposite of what I had before practicing meditation.

A study by John T. Mitchell at Duke University [7] shows that in just eight weeks, 63% of respondents who engaged in "mindfulness meditation" showed a 30% decline in ADHD symptoms like inattention and hyperactive impulses. No one in the control group of non-meditators showed any improvement.

Intuition

Another crucial yet often misunderstood mindfulness concept is tuning into your intuition—also known as following your hunches

---

7   Mitchell, J. T., McIntyre, E. M., English, J. S., Dennis, M. F., Beckham, J. C., & Kollins, S. H. (2017, November). *A pilot trial of mindfulness meditation training for ADHD in adulthood: Impact on core symptoms, executive functioning, and emotion dysregulation.* Journal of attention disorders. https://www.ncbi.nlm.nih.gov/pmc/articles/PMC4045650/

or trusting your gut. The great leaders I work with can all connect to this inner knowing.

Many psychologists believe that your intuition is a kind of pattern-matching between the subconscious and conscious parts of your brain. Here's an example:

You're on the phone with one of your salespeople when a prospect commits to the purchase saying, "I'll confirm with you tomorrow." After the call, you say, "That person won't buy. I can just feel it." A few days go by and sure enough, the order hasn't come through. Your salesperson is amazed and asks for your secret. You don't have a good answer because it's your intuition picking up on subconscious clues, something you've been honing for 20 years. Maybe it was a wavering in the prospect's voice, maybe they spoke too quickly. Whatever it was, your subconscious noticed it—even when your conscious mind didn't.

Here's another example, involving a near miss for me:

I was invited to be the CEO of an "industry rollup." An industry rollup is when a private equity company gives a whole lot of money to a few people and has them go out and acquire a lot of companies. From there, they form a super company and later sell that for even more money.

It all looked amazing on the outside—the offer was even brought to me by someone I fully trust and respect—but my intuition was telling me it wasn't a good idea. I ended up passing on it even though my ego desperately wanted to do it. After all, what could be more fun, lucrative, and better for my career? It turns out that 90 days after I turned it down, the person financing it pulled the money from the project. By then I would have sold my company and been left in a very complex and difficult situation.

We all have intuition. Often, it can unlock big gains or save you from making bad decisions. Mindfulness and meditation can help to develop it.

Exploration

Perform an experiment. Meditate for five minutes every morning for a week, and see how it goes.

In addition to a meditation practice, how else can you slow down in your life, creating space to become more strategic and impactful? Here are some concrete suggestions:

- When you have a free minute, instead of whipping out your phone and checking email, Facebook, Twitter, the stock market, fantasy football, or the news, give yourself that minute to breathe and re-connect. Just become present. Relax and enjoy the stillness.
- While driving, instead of flipping the dial or hooking up your music player, listen to nothing.
- Give yourself some space just before sleeping and immediately after waking up in the morning. Charge your phone somewhere outside of your bedroom. Don't check it right before bed. Definitely don't check email first thing when you wake up.
- The next time you're bored and stuck in a meeting or a presentation that has lost your attention, focus on who's speaking. See if you can catch their inhalations and exhalations. What else can you learn about them by really focusing?
- Reflect on your life and all the positive things in it. Take a moment to have gratitude and appreciation for your life as a whole.
- Take a common object in your hand. Turn it over. Look at the colors, at what it's made of. See what you can find out about it that you've never noticed before.

- When eating alone, do it like the monks do: focus on eating in silence. Turn off the radio, TV, phone, or computer. Take each bite slowly. Chew your food. Realize how all the flavors mix together. Keep in your mind that food is the fuel for your body, and that it will power you over the next few days.

CHAPTER 4:

Brain Wiring for Leaders

Recently, significant advancements in neuroscience have taught us how the brain is wired. In order to uplevel your mindset, there are several exciting and useful principles about the brain and nervous system that you as a leader need to know.

The Similarity-Attraction Effect

The old adage that opposites attract isn't exactly true. The fact is, we generally feel more comfortable with people who look, act, talk, and walk like we do. It's called the "Similarity-Attraction Effect"[8] [9].

In the past, people who were similar to us were more likely to be from the same group of people as we were. Therefore they were more likely to help us, and less likely to attack us.

In modern times, people similar to us consciously and subconsciously validate us. *After all,* your brain thinks, *if this person—who is similar to me—is successful, then somehow I must be too.* In other words, we feel okay when we're like someone else who is okay. Putting aside whether it's true, or right or wrong, the fact is we

---

8   McPherson, M., Smith-Lovin, L., & Cook, J. (2001). *Birds of a Feather: Homophily in Social Networks.* Annual Review of Psychology. https://www.annualreviews.org/doi/abs/10.1146/annurev.soc.27.1.415

9   *Similarity-Attraction Effect.* https://psychology.iresearchnet.com/social-psychology/interpersonal-relationships/similarity-attraction-effect/

have internal wiring that causes us to think and feel this way. We naturally feel more comfortable with people who are similar to us.

Of course, this can be problematic when we allow the Similarity-Attraction Effect to make us insular, never meeting or relating with people unlike ourselves. It can close us off to innovation, lead to narrow thinking, and point to unconscious biases which we have to overcome. Leadership today involves being active in fostering a culture of diversity and inclusion, which we'll talk more about later in the book.

What this means is: you—and your teams, and even your company culture—attract what you put out.

If you're angry, resentful, unhappy, gossipy, often late, insecure, and tell little white lies, you'll find out that you're more comfortable with people who are the same. You'll hire people with those qualities. Others like you will see the same in you, so they'll push you up the ladder, and your friends and work circles will tend to be made up of those people.

Just the same, if you're strong in your integrity, driven, sharp, confident, and optimistic, you'll find yourself attracting like-minded people and groups. Like attracts like. That's why it's crucial to be clear and honest about where you are now and do the work to embody positive, strong qualities. As a leader, this neuroscience is something you can actively lean on. When you empower your teams with this, they can help to build the team and company culture with you.

Exploration

Think of people you like to spend the most time with. What do you talk about? What are your shared interests? What do you have in common? How does that relate to where you are now, and where you want to go?

Wiring Works Against Change

Change is a constant for all businesses, and leaders need to be at the forefront of those initiatives. The problem is our brain doesn't like change.

This has to do with your working memory. Working memory is made up of your current ideas, projects, to-dos and anything else that requires conscious thought. Various studies[10] dating back to 1956 show that the number of things your working memory can hold is between four and nine.

When you consider everything you need to keep in your head – not just work, but family, diet, fitness, social activities, hobbies, and everything else you have to do – you can see how quickly the available spots in your working memory get filled.

It's a good thing we have something in the brain called the basal ganglia, which along with the prefrontal cortex [11] is in charge of what gets into the working memory. Behaviors that are automatic, like starting your car, making the same breakfast day after day, and fixing your hair don't require space in the working memory. That keeps it free to process thoughts and actions that need conscious attention. When we institute change, it can overload the working memory, sometimes called cognitive overload, and cause stress[12].

What does this mean for leading change in an organization? If someone in your accounting department has been following the

---

10   Cowan, N. (2010). The magical mystery four: How is working memory capacity limited, and why? Current directions in psychological science. https://www.ncbi.nlm.nih.gov/pmc/articles/PMC2864034/#R12

11   McNab, F., & Klingberg, T. (2007). Prefrontal cortex and basal ganglia control access to working memory. Nature News. https://www.nature.com/articles/nn2024

12   MPG. (2014). Information overload: Memory and focus are at risk. Morris Psychological Group. https://morrispsych.com/information-overload-memory-and-focus-are-at-risk/

same accounts receivable process for the last 10 years, they're used to doing these tasks in a repetitive, automatic way. Then, when you want to implement a new, state-of-the-art enterprise software system, they'll have to upend their whole process and significantly start using their working memory, which will be noticeably harder for them.

Trying to change anything the basal ganglia is doing automatically is uncomfortable, and people will consciously and subconsciously resist, shifting into the ego. That's why driving change is so hard, especially for people who aren't used to it, because they like their working memory exactly where it is.

Exploration

Where in your role are you leading or managing change? Reflect on how those initiatives are going, and how the people involved are faring. Are you giving everyone the support they need? Remember, people may not be voicing or showing their concerns. You may have to investigate.

What the Need for Belonging Means for Teams

Since the beginning of time, safety meant being part of a small group of other humans—something we have a lot of names for like family, clan, or tribe. If we weren't accepted by the group, or we got thrown out to fend for ourselves, we would most likely die. Sociologists often point out that living in groups is the defining characteristic that makes us human. That's why we have such a need to be accepted, and for our tribe to do well, because if we don't, we might perish. All human brains are wired to seek acceptance from groups—people want to belong.

Unfortunately, it turns out humans will do questionable things, or sacrifice their own values because of group pressure. Have you ever been asked—or have you ever asked someone—to change the numbers on a report? Maybe you know of scenarios where the sales manager gave instructions to lie to a prospective client? How about the time a group went to the strip club at the yearly conference, and it was assumed you and everyone else would lie to your spouses? This is the core need for belonging in effect.

Take a moment to consider the groups you're in, and ask yourself where the need to belong is impacting people. It can take real discipline to be true to oneself when others in the group, especially the leaders, have a different set of values. This is important brain science that you can make work for you as a leader. One way is to get clear about your values and communicate them with your team, which we'll cover later in the book. This will attract like-minded people who feel strongly about the team because of the match in values. This affinity creates strong bonds, high levels of trust, and synergy as team members work together. When you use what you know about building belonging and safety in this way, you'll be astonished at the empowerment that results. People who have access to a feeling of safety and belonging can grow into amazing team members and human beings.

Now you know why culture and values, when done right, can drive a lot of positive behavior without micromanaging—once they're ingrained.

Exploration

Are you utilizing people's desire for belonging in a positive way, to create culture, bonding, and enjoyment? What else could you implement to bring people closer together? Who is suffering from a lack of belonging and how can you influence that?

Change Your Brain via Neuroplasticity

It's estimated that 90 to 95% of your thoughts and behaviors are due to either nature—what's in your DNA due to genetic programming—or nurture—behavior you learned from your parents in your upbringing. What you do each day, and how you show up as a leader is due to what you were born with or how you were brought up. Pre-programmed.

However, thanks to advances in brain science, we now know that 100% of that is changeable. Our brains are neuroplastic, and we can shape them. Sorry, that means no more blaming mom or dad for where you're at. Who you are, how you act and how you think—your mindset—are in your control, and you can change all of it. This is critical information you can use to evolve as a leader. And of course, that means you can help your team do the same.

Here's an overview of how to rewire your brain:

Neurons are the fundamental units of our brain and nervous system. They are the cells responsible for receiving sensory input from the external world, for sending motor commands to our muscles, and for transforming and relaying the electrical signals at every step in between.

The brain's ability to adapt and change is known as neuroplasticity, and its capacity to do this is staggering. There's a saying that's taught on the first day of every neuroscience program: *"Neurons that fire together wire together."* Simply put, this means that if you do things over and over, your brain changes. That's how you change your habits and how you think. It really is that simple.

When you think about leading, and evolving your mindset, remember that your brain changes through repetition. This probably isn't news to you—but it's one thing to just repeat things, and another thing to consciously choose to create new habits and actions by tapping into the power of your brain's plasticity. If you ever get stuck and want to know how to get unstuck, take a moment to intentionally pick a new action, then repeat it the right way over and over. You're creating new neuronal pathways each time you do that.

Psychology and neuroscience are a powerful pair, which we're making the most of in this book. Think of psychology as identifying the thought patterns and beliefs you want to change and healing the core issues, then think of neuroscience as reprogramming a thought pattern through focused repetition. If this is new to you, it may sound a bit mechanical at first. After all, it's not commonly spoken about, especially as it relates to being the best leader possible. Right now you're just learning the essentials. Now you know enough about how your brain works to create new levels of results. In the next chapters, you'll learn much more about the practical applications.

Exploration

Do you have a designated time in your day when you work on reprogramming your brain? The best time is often said to be just after a morning meditation, but the real best time is whenever you'll actually follow through.

You'll learn more techniques for reprogramming as you go through this book that you'll be able to work into your daily routine.

CHAPTER 5:

Confidence, Resilience and Presence

Think of a leader you look up to. It can be a leader from the world of business, sports, religion, politics, or even from your local community. Do you remember a time when you met that person in real life, or maybe heard them speak? Would you consider them confident? That's one trait that every successful leader has—they're confident in some area. After all, when's the last time you saw an insecure leader and thought *I want to follow them?*

My team and I performed an in-depth study in 2019 where we dove into what holds leaders back. After engaging with over 250 leaders from around the world and conducting over 100 hours of research, the number one mindset trait that held them back was lack of confidence.

Confidence doesn't mean you need to know all the answers; it doesn't mean you have a plan for everything. Confidence is strong inner belief, trusting who you are, where you're going, and that you'll find a way to make things work.

When I talk about confidence, many people tell me they don't want to be arrogant. That's because they have the wrong idea about confidence.

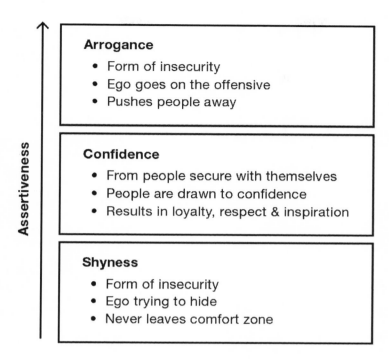

Figure 7: Window of Confidence

Figure 7: Window of Confidence shows how assertiveness plays out in different leaders. If someone isn't assertive enough that's shyness. It's the ego trying to hide and play small. On the other extreme, too much assertiveness shows up as arrogance. Arrogance is also a function of ego; arrogant people go on the offensive so that people don't see the real them. Deep down they don't believe in themselves, and they don't want to connect to others, as that may mean they get found out as a fraud. Arrogance is a disguise for fear.

In the middle is this amazing Window of Confidence. Great leaders need to be assertive when necessary; standing up for their values, holding people accountable, and declaring the vision and purpose. However, they also know when to let other people take responsibility and when to take a back seat.

This confidence comes from the authentic self, and it's what people are drawn to. It's what creates loyalty and respect and what inspires others. This confidence is so magnetic that I've seen staff follow leaders from company to company to company.

Exploration

We'll work on confidence, resilience, and self-esteem in different parts of the book. For now, just answer these questions to gain more awareness. This will assist you as you read on.

Where and when are you shy? What is your ego trying to hide you from?

Where can you get defensive or be arrogant? Why does the ego think that's needed?

Resilience in Leadership

One of the toughest aspects of leadership is the number of decisions you have to make, usually with limited information, all with potentially huge consequences. That's why some managers get burnt out—not because of overwork but because they don't have the internal capacity to handle the level of responsibility and pace that comes with the position. They get so stressed that their mental health suffers, affecting not only themselves and their team, but their family and other people close to them.

Leaders need to be extremely resilient in order to bounce back from difficult situations and to implement new initiatives, all while keeping the team morale and energy up. Resilience is an extension of your confidence and self-esteem. When things are tough, there will be times where you'll need to carry your team on your back and let people know—based on how you're showing up—that everything is going to be alright.

In the last few years, I've worked with a lot of boards and owners who had to address their teams during times of crisis. I taught them that *each and every single time* they were in front of their people, they needed to have hope and positivity. There's enough chaos and uncertainty in people's lives; can you imagine if your leader showed up defeated and directionless? People would lose faith and hope instantly.

That doesn't mean you need to lie, nor does it mean you have to be "rah-rah"—artificially positive—all the time. It's OK to say you don't know the answer; it's even OK to let people know you don't yet have a plan. What they need to hear—and *feel*—is that you have total confidence that together you'll get through it.

Exploration

What image do you portray to your team? What image do you want to portray to your team?

Do you feel you need more resilience? In what areas?

From the Inside Out

Recently, I was teaching a three-day leadership course in Dubai to an international group of executives. On the second day, as we were getting ready to start the afternoon session, I asked if there were any questions. A gentleman in the back raised his hand.

"Michael, I like everything that we're learning so far, but when are we going to learn about how to lead other people? All you've taught us so far is how to get to know ourselves."

What a great question. And I'll tell you the same thing I told him.

Yes, there are some things in leadership that are about how to interact with others—like how to have difficult conversations, how to motivate and inspire, and how to hold people accountable (All of which were covered later in that course, and you'll learn here as well.) However, the core of great leadership has to do with *who you are being.*

After all, your leadership is a reflection of your relationship with yourself.

That's why we always focus on you as the leader first. Just like when you coach and mentor the leaders under you, you'll have them focus on themselves first.

This is about knowing exactly who you are, what you stand for, what your role is, and what your value is. Then it's about standing powerfully in that space to empower others. It's not about getting caught up in politics, judgments, negativity, complaining, excuses, self-limiting beliefs, or anything else. It's about being in your authentic self.

In other words, it's an inside-out job.

In my 20s, there were two people I looked up to: Bruce and George, my mentors. If Bruce talked a certain way, I tried to talk the same way. If George ran a meeting a certain way, I tried to do the same. And it went over horribly because I wasn't Bruce or George. After a while I realized that trying to *be them* wasn't working. I needed to figure out who I was, and fast.

Because I wasn't connected internally to who I was, I wasn't liked or trusted, even though my numbers and performance were excellent. This went on for a while. But once I learned the why, when I understood *why* Bruce said something, and *why* George ran a meeting that way, I was able to run that through the filter of *my own* personality, my authentic self—and that's when I started to flourish.

It takes courage to be you and to be fully present. That's what people are attracted to and respond to in their leaders. It may not feel natural at first, so you'll have to have a little trust. Keep following along and we'll get you there.

> ## Exploration
>
> Think about the leadership challenges you have with other people right now. What can you change about yourself and your own approach? (Keep in mind you can only control yourself, never someone else…)
>
> Reflect on your role models and people you look up to. Are you trying to be exactly like them? Take their best qualities and visualize those in yourself, then let them play out naturally for you, through your authentic self.

The Myths of Vulnerability & Authenticity

There's so much talk about how leaders should be more authentic and vulnerable. But the people saying that are creating more issues. While it's true that leaders who are vulnerable and authentic are more trusted, more respected, and ultimately more successful[13], vulnerability and authenticity are byproducts of being more confident and having more self-esteem.

You can't simply tell someone to be more authentic and vulnerable, just as you can't tell someone to be more handsome, likeable, or funny.

If you take someone currently struggling with their confidence and tell them to be vulnerable and authentic, the results can be damaging and leave the leader and team in a worse place than they were before. There's a healthy, powerful way to be vulnerable, and an unhealthy, unattractive way to be vulnerable.

---

13   Shaffer, E. & Neal, S. (2021). Why leaders must connect more during times of crisis. Catalyst. https://www.catalyst.org/research/leaders-connect-during-crisis/

You know now that your leadership is a reflection of the relationship you have with yourself. That's why we're going to support you in nurturing an exceptional relationship with yourself, so you get to know, like, and trust yourself. So many other things—like vulnerability and authenticity—will fall right into place as a result.

The best place to start is to talk about self-worth.

Self-Worth

I define self-worth as the level of achievement, success, and happiness your ego thinks you're worthy of. This means if you have high self-worth, you'll feel that you could thrive as a director, CEO, or owner of a large company. If you have low self-worth, you'll feel that you don't "deserve" to make a lot of money, get promoted, or have a happy life.

Your actual achievements and level of self-worth will always try to equal out. When your present achievements are higher than your self-worth, you'll experience insecurity, imposter syndrome, and self-sabotage. And when there's a gap between what you subconsciously believe you're worthy of and what you're doing, one (or both) will try to shift.

For example, say you're doing well in your job. You were performing, you had a good team, and you felt confident. Your ego was happy because you were doing something you were comfortable with. Your self-worth was equal to your current achievement.

Things are moving along fine, but then one day, you got promoted. You wanted this promotion, applied for it, and are excited about it.

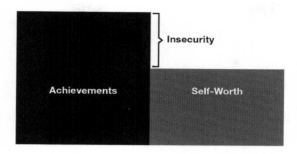

Figure 8: Self-Worth & Achievements - Insecurity

Now that you've increased your status, there's a gap between your achievements and your self-worth. This gap is insecurity (Figure 8). Your promotion brought with it more demand for achievement, but your self-worth hasn't caught up. This imbalance triggers your ego and gets your inner critic to start chirping:

Can I really do this – the promotion is a pretty big deal. I'm not so sure I'm up for it.

I feel like everyone is watching me to see how I do.

Are they waiting for me to fail?

Maybe they think I'm not the right person for this position. Oh no, what if I'm not...

Natural forces try to close the gap. You blindly start to micro-manage, try to control everything, and then you start second-guessing yourself.

If things work out, after a few weeks, you prove to yourself (and your ego) that you can do this new job. With a little time, you sort things out, and things start to work again. Your self-worth catches up to your achievements, and you're back in your authentic self. All is good.

But what if instead, you get another promotion, this time a HUGE one, or you start a company and it scales quickly? What if, for whatever reason, you don't raise your self-worth to catch up to your achievements?

You'll do one of a few things. First, you could self-sabotage. This is the ego's sneaky way of bringing you back to the status quo. This may take the form of getting sick (which happens more than you may think), making bad decisions so you either get demoted or don't get further promoted, blaming other people or factors for your lack of success, or telling yourself you don't even want the role.

Some people get so used to being in their ego, applying old-school top-down leadership from a place of insecurity—it becomes their everyday mode of operation. I see this often in older leaders and in fact I call it the Experienced Leader's Curse, which you'll learn more about in an upcoming chapter.

For now, the most healthy, powerful move you can make is to create a great sense of self-worth. Again, this isn't arrogant or ego-based. It's having faith in yourself. It's improving your relationship to yourself so your leadership can grow from that fertile soil.

When you build self-worth, self-esteem, and confidence, you'll also have natural resilience. You'll find it effortless to exude your magnetic personality so that people trust you and want to promote and follow you. But the best thing of all—you will find that, since both aspects are always seeking to equal out, your achievements will run to catch up with your self-worth – see Figure 9. When you tap into this kind of human behavior, you'll find yourself much more successful overall.

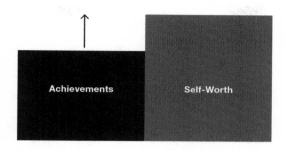

Figure 9: Self-Worth & Achievements - Secure & Confident

Exploration

Do you ever feel that you're not worthy of, or don't deserve something? It could be a promotion, the amount of money you're making, or a leadership role.

Remember it's the ego that's uncomfortable in that moment; it's creating negative self-talk because you're in a state of growth.

Now that you've completed the introduction section, it's time to step through the phases of the Growth Leadership Path. Among many other new mindset shifts, going through the path will build up your confidence, self-worth, and self-esteem.

Before we get to all that building up though, we have to start by clearing what's holding you back.

The Growth Leadership Path

Phase 1:
Release and Reset

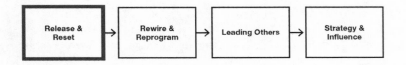

That fateful day on April 1ˢᵗ when my business partner punched me, which you read about in the introduction, caused me to spiral. After reporting the assault to the police, I had to arrange to have an armed security guard posted at my office when I handed my soon-to-be-ex business partner a restraining order and a termination letter—the first of many documents in our coming lawsuit. (I could still fire him since I was the majority owner.)

As my employees arrived for work, I had to explain to each one how the guy who was in business with me, the same person many of them reported to, physically hit me—and that's why he was no longer part of the company.

Then I had to call each one of our clients, many of whom had known him for years, and were used to dealing with him as their main point of contact. I had to let them know he was no longer with us. When they asked why he'd left so suddenly, I gave them vague answers because I thought the details were best left out.

Exhausted from the emotional toll of the day, when I got home, I collapsed onto the sofa. I was on the verge of once again escaping reality through drinking and drugs, but that evening I began to take stock of my life, instead. My mind began to race:

I'm working so hard, and in some ways I'm succeeding. After all, the current issue with my business partner aside, the business has had some success.

But am I happy? Have I been happy? Will I be happy?

No, no, and probably not.

Am I creating a lasting business? Do people respect me? Am I building a company that I'm proud of? Do I feel in control…of anything? What am I even working towards?

The more questions I asked, the less I was satisfied with the answers.

Why? I had big goals, I was achieving some of them, yet I was getting less happy and fulfilled, not more. It's like I was cursed or broken. After all, I saw other people living a happy and relaxed life, even highly-successful, high-performing people. What was I doing wrong?

That's when I decided to change my goals. Instead of focusing on the amount of money I was bringing in, the size of my business, and trying to earn people's respect, I told myself I needed to find out more about myself and how to create a better life for myself.

If not, I thought I might just end up dead.

That's when I found the perfect place to do just that; the University of Santa Monica and their Spiritual Psychology Master's program. Yes, that's right—the Psychology degree I hold is actually a Masters in *Spiritual* Psychology. What makes it "spiritual" psychology?

It has nothing to do with religion—rather, it takes a humanistic view of psychology. We learned six different modes of psycho-analysis—Behavioral, Person-Centered/Rogerian, Gestalt, Rational-Emotive, NLP, and Psychosynthesis—and how to apply them through a lens of pure compassion and love.

Spiritual psychology teaches us how to move out of our ego and into our authentic self. When we get stuck in our ego, it's because we have an unresolved psychological issue, and we can use one or a combination of the six therapeutic techniques mentioned above to heal and clear ourselves of that issue. Then we're more in line with our true, authentic selves—our soul, if you choose to believe we have a soul.

Much of what you're learning in this book was born out of what I learned through that program.

The degree was life changing—the most profound healing I've ever done in my life by far. What I learned was that I was holding onto a lot that I needed to let go. Until I did, I would never break out of the cycle I was in.

Remember our definition of leadership, that it's a reflection of your relationship with yourself? In this following chapters, we're going to clear your long-standing, subconscious blocks and make fundamental changes to your relationship with yourself.

CHAPTER 6:

Blindspots, Blocks and Beliefs

As I hung up the phone, I thought to myself, *wow, what an amazing referral – that's a huge piece of business that could double or triple our revenue this year.*

Someone in my network had just called and let me know that a large company was actively looking for the exact type of software system that we sold. You'd assume I would call them immediately in order to start the sales process.

Instead, I was blocked, and rather than jump on the opportunity, I procrastinated and waited a few days to reach out. Subconsciously my fear was holding me back.

What if they say my company is too small to serve them? Or ask me complex questions I can't answer?

The thought of doubling or tripling our revenue was overwhelming. My ego was playing tricks on me and I didn't feel worthy of growing that much, that fast. Clearly, if I wanted to get beyond where I was, I had to release this blindspot right away.

Over the next few chapters you're going to discover all the hidden ways that leaders, and people in general, hold themselves back. Many people who attend my trainings and masterminds profess that this is the most powerful content I teach. Because these blocks are subconscious, we need to look at them from a few different angles to uncover and eventually overcome them.

In the book *The Big Leap,* psychologist Gay Hendricks examines a phenomenon he calls the upper limit problem—an invisible ceiling that your ego doesn't want you to surpass. That's why smart, driven, capable people seem to get stuck at a certain level.

Maybe you quickly climbed the career ladder early on, but when you look at the last few years, you've lost that upward momentum. You've been comfortable doing fairly well in the same position for a while. Or the business, division, or team that you've grown seems to have plateaued, and nothing you've tried has resulted in that continued growth you previously enjoyed. That's because your subconscious ego is happy with where you're at right now and is holding you back from the next step.

Here are a few more ways you may be hitting your upper limit:

Have you ever had something important coming up—a performance, interview, presentation, or a speech—and something happened that threw a spanner in the works? Maybe you got sick, lost your keys, or missed your flight?

These are often cases of self-sabotage. Make no mistake, your ego can make you physically sick in order to bypass something it's not sure about. After all, there's no limit to what it will do in order to make sure it's keeping some measure of control!

How many times have you had an important call or meeting—but you had to answer that one last email or do one last thing, that wound up almost making you late and forcing you to rush? That's your ego at work as well. It's subconscious, but it's there.

Here's a good one. Have you ever been around someone you really admire, or find attractive, but when you go up to them, you're so tongue-tied that you sound like an idiot? That's your ego telling you that you're not worthy of having this extremely attractive person also attracted to you!

Another way to break this down is this: everyone has a comfort zone. That's where life is good, easy, comfortable. As leaders, we're naturally pushed out of our comfort zone – it's just the nature of leadership. We have to lead change, have difficult conversations, take responsibility for new and challenging projects.

When you move out of your comfort zone, your ego kicks in. As you've learned, your ego hates being in new situations, taking risks, and not being sure of the outcome. So, it does its best to come up with reasons to protect you. Its sole goal at this point is to make you so uncomfortable that you run back to your comfort zone.

This can take the form of procrastination (*I'm not going to start until I know I can be perfect*), insecurity (*oh my gosh I'm going to fail*), comparison *(there are much smarter and more experienced people than me)*, the previously mentioned imposter syndrome *(someone's going to find out I don't know what I'm doing),* and a whole host of other tactics.

That inner chatter can be never-ending—but it's something you can release.

Exploration

Do you self-sabotage or compare yourself to others? Do you suffer from imposter syndrome? Are you aware of any blindspots? Take a moment to reflect on what causes these things in your life, and the circumstances in which they occur.

CHAPTER 7:

The Origins of Self-Limiting Beliefs

Self-limiting beliefs are exactly what they sound like: beliefs that hold you back. They are the reason that the upper limit problem exists. These ideas that we accept without doubt usually exist on the subconscious level, so you don't even know they're there. Those sneaky little devils are great at hiding—and finding all sorts of ways to sabotage the things you're trying to achieve.

To discover your limiting beliefs, consider these questions:

- Do you find yourself compelled to work all the time?
- Does it sometimes feel like you attract drama into your life?
- Do you experience a lot of guilt?
- Do you make self-sabotaging decisions that hold you back?
- Are you so goal-oriented that you live life always chasing the next achievement?
- Are you searching for a more stable, loving relationship with your spouse, partner or kids?
- Have you hit a plateau in business, life or in your relationships?
- Do you procrastinate?
- Are you constantly busy and harried?
- Do you wonder what it's going to take before you're happy and fulfilled?

If you answered "yes" to any of these questions, the root cause is subconscious beliefs. Everyone has them, and each and every one can be overcome.

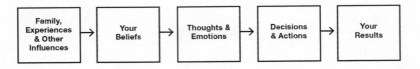

Figure 10: The causes and effects of Self-Limiting Beliefs

Figure 10 shows how your experiences and influences determine your beliefs, which shape your thoughts and emotions, which determine your decisions and actions, which lead to the results in your life.

In this chapter, we're going to look at the sources of self-limiting beliefs. For each source you'll find some questions to consider, which will give you your first insight into your beliefs. In the next chapter, you'll learn the most common limiting beliefs that show up for leaders. This will allow you to identify more of your own beliefs. Then we'll also cover a quick and easy way to make progress toward overcoming your limiting beliefs.

When I teach this module in my Leadership Masterminds, every single person gets deep insights about themselves. If you're interested in learning what can get you to the next level—and the next level after that—this is the area to focus on. Let's start with getting to the origins of subconscious, self-limiting beliefs.

Intergenerational

The number one source of your behaviors and beliefs is your family. Parents and caregivers have by far the greatest impact on your beliefs as you're growing up. We call these intergenerational self-limiting beliefs.

Before we discuss how to change some of these beliefs and behaviors, keep in mind that much of what you've learned from your parents as role models is valuable. For example, when I look back to see what I gained from my family, I know I learned to work hard, to be honest, active in the community, entrepreneurial, and many other foundational things. You want to keep and honor those positive behaviors rather than throw them out, and tease out what's not serving you. Or you may have a thought pattern that's helpful in one part of your life but not another.

It can be helpful, too, to remember that this is not an exercise in digging up the past and figuring out who to blame for what's wrong in your life. In many cases, the beliefs we pick up, particularly from our parents, reflect their concern for us. This means that even though we learned limiting beliefs from them, in most cases their intentions were to equip us well for life, and for whatever reason it created a belief that is now not serving us. Sometimes this occurred because of their insecurities, other times it's because of the situation or a need to survive. Whatever the reason, that's not very important. What is important is identifying and creating new, more authentic, powerful beliefs.

Finally, keep in mind that although you inherited some of your beliefs, every single belief and behavior can be changed using the neuroscience we covered earlier. Don't use your past to justify being a victim in the present. Focus on the beliefs that are holding you back and engage the processes you'll learn in this chapter.

Right now, picture your mother, father, or someone else who brought you up:

- What was their attitude towards work?
- What was their attitude towards money and success?
- Do you consider them happy?

Now, how is your attitude towards money, work, and success similar or <u>opposite</u> to theirs? Sometimes we see a behavior in our parents and we make a commitment to never get caught in that trap ourselves. We say, "This is never going to happen to me."

For example, if someone had a parent who was always embarrassing themselves, that child might work hard to make sure they never embarrass themselves in public. They may take this to an obsessive degree, so much so that they feel inhibited in public and end up missing opportunities as a result. What's more, they may also judge people who make a spectacle of themselves in public, whether intentionally or otherwise.

Or, let's say you had a parent who spent way more money than they had, which caused issues because bills weren't paid or there was always credit card debt. As a result, you might watch every penny—even if you have millions in your bank account.

Maybe you had an overbearing grandparent, and as a child you were conditioned to always be quiet and not draw attention to yourself so that you wouldn't get yelled at. That may play out now as reluctance to speak up when you have something valuable to say. It may also make you afraid to stand out from the crowd, and keep you from jumping into the fray when an opportunity presents itself.

Exploration

To start identifying your intergenerational patterns, take some time now to reflect on your family. Think back to the parents and caregivers who had a role in your upbringing and answer these questions for each:

- What was their attitude towards work and money?
- Did they make a lot of money? Or not much?
- Did they hate or love their jobs?

- Were they frugal, watching every penny—or did they overspend, saddled with debt?
- Did they admire successful, wealthy people, or did they view them with suspicion and resentment?
- Does your family talk openly about money, even now, in a healthy way?

Once you've given these questions some thought, consider: how do the answers relate to you? And as you do that, list out both what you consider "negative" beliefs (ones that hold you back) as well as "positive" ones, as that's a good way to bring in compassion and appreciation within the exercise.

Today, in your life, who and what bothers you? What drives you? When do you experience fear and anxiety? Start mapping your answers back to your family. See if you can connect why you are the way you are right now, back to how you were brought up. This is part of releasing things that hold you back. As you uncover these patterns, you'll have profound realizations about why you think and behave the way you do.

As you explore the questions I've given you, be kind to yourself. Don't judge yourself or get down on yourself—or anyone else in your family. This is a process of self-realization and evolution. I can't even say it's a natural evolution, as most people don't have the opportunity, desire, or courage to look this deeply and to change. So proceed with compassion, kindness, and love for all involved.

Cultural Identity

Another place to look for the source of your limiting beliefs is in the culture you live in, including geographical, religious, racial and even gender influences. These may be broader than the impact from your immediate family, but together they form a kind of extended family that you live within. It's very common to draw at least a portion of our identity from these factors.

Racial Influences

Consider, for example, what behaviors are "normal" for people of your race? Do you generally feel like an outsider, or do you belong? Have you ever had bad service at a restaurant, and wondered if it had something to do with how you look, how you talk, what you're wearing, or how people perceive you? Whether you're treated well, or not, you have likely internalized messages about yourself from how others treat you and have limiting self-beliefs because of that.

On one standardized test, a certain group of people were asked about their race at the beginning of the test, and a second group were not. It was the exact same test, but the group that got asked their race did worse. What race we're talking about isn't relevant, what's important is that this proves our cultural identity—and how we're treated based on it—can hold us back.

Geographic Influences

How about the norms among people from your hometown? Maybe in the neighborhood where you grew up, people with long hair and tattoos were seen as lower class. And if you grew up in the American South or Europe, you most likely have a different set of values and beliefs from someone who grew up in Los Angeles or New York. All of these contribute to self-limiting beliefs in one way or other.

I grew up in Pittsburgh, Pennsylvania, which was once a big steel town when my parents were kids, in the 1950's, 60's and 70's. The people in their neighborhood were blue-collar immigrants, many from Eastern Europe—mine were from Croatia. People either worked in the steel mills or in small businesses supporting the mills and the community. In fact, it was so blue-collar that my parents and relatives told me no one in town would trust someone wearing a business suit. That's what the bosses at the steel mill wore, and there was a big divide between the workers on the floor and the management.

Here then, is a cultural and geographic belief at work—that people in suits can't be trusted.

Imagine that you grew up in that town at that time. Your parents, who worked in the mill, saved and scraped so you could go to university and become a lawyer. You worked for years to get your law degree and get a job with a law firm. The first day of work, what do you need to do? Wear a suit.

What happens now? Your conscious mind doesn't see anything wrong with putting on a jacket and tie. Yet you have this subconscious belief that whoever is wearing one is a crook and a liar. One of a few things could happen next.

Maybe you self–sabotage your law career. You find yourself not fitting in and hating the job. That's because, deep down, your mind and ego are working against you, telling you that the career you've chosen is one that crooks and liars do. Ultimately, you quit and find a job where the dress code is much more casual. Makes sense, right?

Another way that your ego and beliefs could get their way is to have you become sick and have to stop working. You realize that whenever you stay home for a few weeks you get better, but when you go back to the office, it affects you again. Your beliefs are holding you back.

Things could go even worse, and you could come into internal alignment by swinging the other way and live into that identity belief—and become a crook yourself. You become the attorney who will look the other way, lie for their clients, represent criminals, or just overbill and do things that are out of integrity.

You can see how these beliefs work behind the scenes and become hidden obstructions to you becoming that authentic, powerful, highly successful leader that you want to be.

Gender Influences

You may not realize it, but your gender can also affect your belief system—what you think you can and can't do. Especially within a corporate setting, men often feel pressure to be strong, stoic, and unfeeling. Many hold the belief that emotions make them look weak. Women, on the other hand, often feel that they're judged by their looks, their weight, or their femininity. In some cases, women may tie their self-worth to these traits.

Personally, I have to work to be vulnerable and share my feelings. It takes intention and effort to overcome a belief that as a man, I shouldn't ask for help. And I know that women often have to overcome subconscious judgments by others. This no doubt contributes to the "glass ceiling" phenomenon, and to the wage disparities many women encounter, especially when they become leaders.

There are many ways gender biases contribute to beliefs about ourselves and each other. Take a moment to consider how you might be limiting yourself regardless of what gender you identify with.

Religious Influences

The religion you grew up in, or the one that you follow now, may also have formed your beliefs. For example, my family is Catholic, and guilt was a common theme growing up. From colleagues of mine who are Jewish, I understand that there's a cultural tendency to jokingly complain to each other. "You think you have it bad? You should see how bad I have it."

In other religious systems, women are treated differently from men—giving them fewer opportunities and more constraints. Consider for a moment how many religions embrace the concept of martyrdom, where having a tough life—overworking, over giving, people pleasing and other ways of self-sacrificing—can be seen as a kind of honorable suffering. These are places where self-limiting beliefs can emerge.

Of course, these are stereotypes, but it's often very useful to check in on these for yourself. I'm not saying they apply across the board. What I'm saying is far more simple: we often play into the stereotypes of the religion we grew up with, in the same way that we're influenced by our families. If you're Jewish and you tend to complain about life—jokingly or not—did that become part of your identity from your religious background? If you're Catholic, and you tend to feel a lot of guilt, realize that life doesn't have to be that way.

These self-limiting beliefs can also be used as a kind of shorthand for relating to one another. A woman in my family nags a lot. One time I asked her why she does it, and she answered, "Because that's what the women in our family do!" This is an intergenerational, cultural, and gender-based belief—that she has to be a certain way, and she has no intention of changing it. This belief is now part of her identity, and even if it limits her, she's fine with that.

Great leaders use everything they can for their advancement. Everything mentioned here is a clue—information to help you to look at your life with a caring, neutral eye—in service to clearing anything that may be holding you back. Remember, in this section of the Growth Leadership Path, we're releasing the things that are no longer serving us.

Once again I will mention that where you came from, your religion, your family, and every other influence also gave you many great gifts—from honesty to community to family support to resilience to problem solving.

Exploration

As you reflect on these questions, try listing both the negative and positive beliefs you've picked up from each.

When you think of the communities and geographies you've grown up in, what did they deem important and not important? What was acceptable and "cool", and what wasn't?

What are the race, gender and religious influences that have influenced you?

Once you've listed your beliefs, look closely and try to map them back to how that's affecting your life presently.

Situational Influences

The above are examples of things that have shaped you over time since birth. But you may also undergo an isolated experience, or a series of experiences—often traumatic—that lead to self-limiting beliefs.

These could come in the form of:

- You or a close family member getting sick or injured, for example, having to deal with cancer yourself or witnessing a parent or sibling going through the same
- Living through a natural or non-natural disaster, such as a hurricane or earthquake, or even a terrorist attack
- Getting bullied or abused

When I work with people on healing deep and traumatic issues, it's common for them to bring up times when they were young and were picked last at sports. They don't even know that's been causing them to shy away from attention and not put themselves forward. Once they identify and clear the trauma, they see life with new eyes.

People also may, for instance, avoid arguments—even constructive ones—if they were caught in the crossfire of parents' arguments when they were younger. They may feel more than a little nervous around sick people if poor health plagued their childhood. Or, they might go the other way and rush to play the caretaker for someone who's ill, even at the expense of their own health. The rumble of distant thunder might put someone on edge if years ago their house was flooded in a powerful storm. Whatever the case may be, our subconscious minds imprint certain rules in our heads in an effort to protect us—well beyond the end of the traumatic event.

Again, I can't stress enough how important it is to not judge any of these beliefs—or yourself for holding them. Take them in as neutral information. I know we're touching on some deep subjects, issues you've carried inside perhaps for your entire life. As you start uncovering them, remember to have compassion for yourself.

As we've seen, many beliefs are passed on to us from previous generations, or via religion, race, gender, and other influences. Up till now there was little you could do about them. But now that you know about them, you can start to change them.

Remember, too, that there's always more help available to access the deeper work you're starting here. Reach out to a professional or contact me and my firm. We're always here to support you with work at deeper levels, to heal faster, and to get to a better place in your life and work.

Exploration

What major events have occurred in your life? What "agreements" might you have made with yourself (or anyone or anything else) because of those things? How has that shaped you today?

A Common Concern

"But wait, Michael, these beliefs are what made me successful. If I overcome them, what if I lose my edge, my drive?"

This is a legitimate concern that often comes up when people start learning about their self-limiting beliefs and we get ready to clear them. I get it. And don't worry. I can tell you that you'll be much more successful once you've cleared out these beliefs. That's because they take up so much negative energy in your body and mind—they suck up all your vitality. They cause you to operate with blinders on and miss things you would normally see.

I worked with one business owner worth tens of millions of dollars. He was in a great place financially, with his wealth spread across property, stocks, and cash in the bank. Yet every single day he woke up scared he was going to wind up poor, like he and his mother were growing up. That's what drove him.

Do *you* want to be driven by fear your whole life?

It's so much more fun—and sustainable—to be driven by a positive force, rather than running away from fear. Shedding these beliefs won't make you less effective; you will be much *more* effective. You're also going to be more charismatic; people will naturally follow you, and you'll be more driven and successful than ever.

A Personal Story

In my spiritual psychology Master's program, we learned a lot of tools and processes that we first practiced on ourselves, with the added benefit of clearing our own unresolved issues.

In one case we did a genogram, also known as a McGoldrick–Gerson study, a Lapidus schematic, or a family diagram. This is a visual picture of family relationships and history. It's like taking your family tree and then marking down all the substance abuse, divorce and separations, infidelity, enmeshments, and more, in order to map out and identify patterns [14.]

Once you've mapped out these relationships, there's a formula, largely based on birth order, that tells you where to find the patterns that are specific to you.

When I did the process, the formula told me to look at my father and his father. My father was a *failed entrepreneur, an alcoholic, and was married multiple times*. Looking at the genogram, I then saw that *his father* was also a failed entrepreneur, an alcoholic, and was married multiple times.

When I looked at myself, the truth hit me like a ton of bricks. Just like my father, and his father, I was an *entrepreneur with major addictions, and had been divorced once already.* I was falling right in line with these intergenerational patterns. Now that I had the awareness of this pattern—could I choose a different response and overcome this pattern, all with compassion?

There are a handful of ways to do deep release work, and in the case of my father, I chose a simple technique which is accessible enough for you to try for yourself. Even though he passed away 15 years before I went through this process, I wrote a letter to him. Then, I wrote a letter *from* him *to* me on his behalf. I'll share that correspondence, but first I'll give you some background.

My father had a great corporate job until I was five years old, then he quit and started a retail picture framing shop. It struggled so much that after a time the IRS—tax authority in the US—shut his shop down because he accumulated massive debt and hadn't paid taxes for years. During those years, he started to drink more and more, became increasingly distant, and finally he left our family.

---

14   For more information on this powerful process, see the books *Homecoming* and *Family Secrets* by John Bradshaw

I don't remember having much of a relationship with him. After he left, I only talked to him once a year or so. He didn't have much interest in staying in touch with my sister or me. Even though he had died years before, I learned through this process that my beliefs about my father and his relationship with me and our family were affecting me. He was no longer around, but the process of writing these letters was a therapeutic release for me.

To do this, I got into a quiet meditative state. My letter to him was written from my inner child, the one who had to go through my father leaving us and never knowing why. Here are the highlights of the letter:

> *Dad, I love you. Though I'm so confused.*
>
> *You never told me you loved me. You never told me you were proud of me. You never told me much of anything.*
>
> *Why did you leave us?*
>
> *Did I do something wrong? Did my sister?*
>
> *We loved you even though it seemed you hated our family. Why?*
>
> *What could I have done differently?*

It was emotional to write this letter—very emotional. I sat with it for a while. Then, because he couldn't write me back, I took the next step in the process: I wrote a second letter on behalf of him, replying to me.

> *Michael, you got it all wrong.*
>
> *I love you so much. I love your sister so much. I even love your Mom.*
>
> *You didn't do anything wrong and I'm so proud of you.*

I took a risk and started the business, but it struggled.

I'm the father, the husband, the man, and it's my job to provide. And I failed in that.

I'm so embarrassed. I let you all down. That's why I drank and then left. Because I didn't deserve you. I ran away. You all were better off without me.

I'm sorry. Please forgive me. I love you always.

Your Dad.

Even though it was my hand that wrote the reply, I know in my heart that it's the truth. During that process there was a huge shift in myself and a releasing of anger, shame, and self-judgment. The reason for that: I changed my core beliefs.

Prior to doing this release work, deep down I believed that my father didn't love me. This meant I wasn't worthy of love, happiness, or success. I felt abandoned and rejected by the main male figure in my life. I must have been broken, even unlovable. The releasing process taught me that the belief I had was totally wrong. I was able to learn a new belief, one that didn't hold me back.

The truth is that my dad loved me—and my family—so much that he made a huge sacrifice. He thought, wrongly or rightly, that we would be better off without him, so he left. I don't agree with what he did and I wish he did things differently, but I understand it now. And what was the real-life result for me?

After clearing the self-limiting belief that I was unlovable and broken, I knew that my father did love me and made difficult choices in his life to do what he thought was best for me. In the next few weeks I stopped my habitual drinking and drug use. All without any additional programs or other kinds of support; it was all due to identifying and healing the deep beliefs I had been holding onto.

All of this should be giving you a good view of why identifying and clearing self-limiting beliefs is critical to you reaching your potential as a leader, and as a person. In the next few chapters, we'll cover the most common self-limiting beliefs leaders have that cause a great deal of aggravation and failure. This will give you practical and straightforward way to identify which ones you hold, and then we'll go about releasing them.

Remember, every leader has a set of blocks that prevents them from growing and evolving. Not every leader does the work of getting past them.

CHAPTER 8:

Common Self-Limiting Beliefs

Now that we've examined the origins of self-limiting beliefs and learned how these beliefs can show up generally with the upper limit problem, let's look more specifically at the places they show up in our lives. Remember, these beliefs come in all shapes, sizes, and variations, so what I put forward here is a guide for you to reveal your own.

I've been affected by each and every one of these beliefs, and almost everyone I've coached has too. If you're reading through and think that they don't apply to you, that's likely your ego doing its best to trick you.

Clients have told me that they enjoy the insights they get as they learn about these beliefs in the moment, and as time passes, they identify even deeper connections between their beliefs and their thoughts, actions, and current situation.

What's great is when you do identify, release, and rewire a belief, the experience can be incredibly liberating. You know it's been holding you back and you get to experience the freedom of letting it go.

Work = Success

The first belief that holds people back is this: You must work hard to be successful. Don't misunderstand this one—hard work can often lead to success. But often people think that they have to go hand-in-hand; success *only* comes with hard work. Why is that a problem?

Personally, I want to be massively successful—*without* a ton of work. There was a time when I was running my largest software company and I achieved the entrepreneur's holy grail; I had a solid management team in place, we were making good money, and I hardly needed to be around the office at all. I could cut my working time down to a day or two a week.

So what did I do? Go and play golf? Relax and enjoy my success? No.

Here's where my belief held me back. I felt guilty making that much money while others were working long hours, so I found reasons to stick around the office. I made up projects and filled up my task list when I didn't need to. What's crazy is that my team was fine with me taking off and being out of the office. They took a lot of pride in fulfilling their roles and knew what I had gone through to get the business to this level.

Deep down I didn't feel I was worthy of that success if I wasn't out there sweating with everyone else. It's like I was resisting what I worked so long and hard for. At various points in my career, I used to try to prove my self-worth by working more hours than everyone else. I was already successful, but I kept trying to earn my place.

Many of us have this belief—that you must work hard to be successful—especially when we come from lower, working, or middle-class blue-collar families. When our role models work and hustle for an hourly wage, we tend to equate working more with more income. Or maybe your ancestors were farmers or small business owners and needed to work incredibly hard to get by.

A strong work ethic is an admirable quality. Almost all success is due to commitment, focus, and hard work. You also have to be clear about when it's serving you and when it's not. When did it become heroic to work 60-hour weeks? Why do we glamorize that over effectiveness? Your self-worth *is not* tied to how many hours you work or how much you sacrifice.

Exploration

If you're always working excessive hours and making sacrifices in other areas of your life, you need to uplevel your leadership mindset. Consider some of the other ways this belief shows up in our lives:

- Do you find it hard to respect someone in a position of authority if they haven't done your job or come from where you have?
- Do you feel guilty when you go on vacation, leave work earlier than others, or have to miss work to go to a doctor's appointment?
- Do you ever look at someone who's successful, or who's won the lottery, and think, *they don't deserve that?*
- Do you get stressed when there's NOT that much on your calendar or to-do list? Are you addicted to being busy?
- Do you hesitate to take more than a day or two off— and when you do, do you still check your emails every day?
- Do you believe that there's no such thing as a free lunch, or that if it's too easy, it can't be real?

Answer each of these questions honestly and start to notice where this belief might be playing out in your life. Can you picture yourself being successful and *not* working hard? I'm not talking about when you make it someday; I'm talking about imagining that happening today. Because you know what? It's possible. And you deserve it.

This is a very common belief among leaders, and once you release it, you'll start making different decisions, setting boundaries, and subconsciously open yourself up to a whole new world of possibilities.

Success Trade-Offs

A few years ago, my phone rang—it was my sister calling. She and her husband had recently bought an independent retail pharmacy. She was telling me that work was going well, although she felt she wasn't spending enough time with the kids. She would go back and forth on this. One day the family was good but the business was struggling, and the next time we spoke she'd tell me that while business was good, there were issues with her family.

I asked her, "Ami, you do realize that it's possible to be successful in your business AND have a great family life as well?"

There was a long silence. I thought the connection had dropped. Then she said "No…deep down, I never thought that was possible."

The belief that there are trade-offs we must make in our lives comes from our upbringing. Do you recall from my previous story that my father was around for a few years, and when he started a business, our family fell apart? In this conversation, it became clear that my sister was playing into those same patterns.

Ask yourself: if you're successful, what do you expect that to "cost" you—your family life, your health, vacations, happiness, being in shape, your inner peace, your femininity or masculinity, your soul, or something else entirely?

A woman from Romania once heard me speak at an event, and we sat down to talk a week later. She explained to me that her family holds an intergenerational belief that if someone becomes successful, they'll get sick. Not cold or flu sick, but cancer and leukemia sick. The belief here is that success requires sacrifice, giving up, trading something, or enduring something in return.

Do you ever look at wealthy and successful people and get jealous? Maybe you think they must have inherited their fortune, or had to lie and cheat or sacrifice their family life to get it, and that's why they're where they are—and you're not? I used to find myself jealous and resentful of wealthy people for reasons like these. I felt that if I was going to be successful I'd have to compromise my own ethics. This was a purely self-limiting belief. Eventually I realized that I would never become wealthy with that mindset.

This belief shows up many different ways. Maybe you think that because you lead the team, or you're the boss, you also have to be the one who takes on the dirty jobs? If someone has to work on a weekend, do you think it's your duty to do it? In your view, does the captain always go down with his ship? Do you always have to be the one to make the sacrifice and "do your time?"

There's a word for people like this: martyr. Someone who does difficult work, often the work no one else wants, in order for their ego to feel satisfied. Maybe this gives them bragging rights around the office or a sense of satisfaction through self-inflicted punishment. Either way, it's not a healthy driver.

Keep an eye out, not just for you, but make sure your team avoids getting caught in the martyr trap, self-sacrificing as a tradeoff for success. Even though they may be working a lot of hours and picking up a lot of people's slack, this often leads to burn out, resentment, passive aggressiveness, and causes divisions between team members.

Of course, it's not necessarily bad to work weekends now and again, or to raise your hand and volunteer to work with the large, arrogant client that everyone hates. Just as in the Work = Success equation, it's not that work and success aren't related. There are times when it makes sense to forego something pleasurable in order to get something done.

Rather, it's your energy around the decision and the thoughts driving your efforts. If you're always waiting for something to happen before you're happy and successful, and time after time sacrifice your boundaries to try to get ahead, then that's where the problem is.

Exploration

Here are some additional questions to help you explore this limiting belief:

- Do you doubt that you can truly have it all? That you can be successful at work and still have a happy home life? Be successful and in good physical shape? Be successful and healthy?
- Do you play the martyr or victim?
- Do you believe that because you're the boss you have to take on the worst jobs? Do you pride yourself on your sacrifices?
- Do you have obligations in your life that you don't enjoy but think they're your duty? Are you doing them because you feel you should be doing them, rather than questioning whether they need to be done?
- Are you waiting to be happy or to think better of yourself until something in particular happens? Examples: until you get a new job, write that book, save enough money for retirement, etc.

- Do you believe that wealthy people are cheats and liars, are somehow unhappy and unfulfilled, or that they hold some other negative trait?

For each question you answered "Yes" to, take some time to explore that. What could be the sources of that belief? How is it holding you back? If that's an untrue belief, what's the truth?

Obligation. Duty. Sacrifice. These are all words that, in certain situations, can have undertones of victimhood and entitlement. Is that what's driving your life? To get to your next level of leadership, are you ready to let that go?

Lack of Worthiness

A friend and I were having coffee the other day, and after watching an interaction a few feet away in which someone was clearly bragging, she said, "One of the things I hate the most is when people are arrogant."

I thought about that for a second, and I told her, "Arrogance isn't my favorite trait either, but what I really dislike is when people don't own their own power—when they don't embrace the gifts, skills, and abilities they already have."

How many people do you know who are great at something but hide and play it safe?

Maybe they're an amazing singer or piano player but never want to sing or play around anyone. Or they're an amazing artist, a great writer, or have an idea for a business, yet never move forward with that. Or they don't put their name up for promotion when they're clearly a good candidate for advancement. These people play small when the world needs them to play big. They lack a sense of their own value, of their own inherent worth.

THAT lack of taking action bugs me a heck of a lot more than arrogance.

After all, how would the world be if everyone had the confidence to use their talents without apologizing, hiding, or running from their own power? That's right, the world would be even more amazing…yet so few people are owning their self-worth.

This plays out in so many areas. For example, when someone compliments you, do you deflect? When someone says, "Great job," how do you reply?

"Nah, it was no big deal."

"It was the team, not me."

"I got lucky."

"Oh, I'm just blessed."

Or do you look them in the eyes and say a sincere "Thank you?"

I hereby give you permission—from now until the end of time—to take in compliments and accept them WITHOUT deflecting or feeling guilty.

That's not arrogance, that's acknowledging a kind word and accepting someone else's gift.

Remember that the Growth Leadership Path is a journey of strengthening your self-esteem. Hiding from your worthiness moves you away from that. Being honest about your gifts, skills, and abilities brings you closer to who you are. It is, in fact, a matter of integrity—with yourself and with others.

There's a (made-up) story about a doctor who retired to a small, rural town. He didn't tell anyone he was a doctor as he didn't want to stand out or seem like he was bragging. Not too long after he arrived a young girl next door became ill, but the family didn't know this man was a doctor, so they never asked him for help—and the girl died.

I've seen talented person after talented person pass up opportunities because they weren't confident enough to say, "Yes, I can do it—or at least give it my best try."

If I put you in front of a group of strangers and they asked you what you were good at, what would you say? What if I told you all to form a team, and someone asked if you wanted to be the leader of the team?

The real inquiry is—when you consider the questions I posed above, what happens within you? What does your inner voice say?

A big growth moment for me was at an event for business owners several years ago. We all sat at tables of eight people each. Many of the people at my table were older and ran larger companies than I did, and none of us knew each other personally. The facilitator told each table to choose a leader. We started by awkwardly glancing at each other. Someone started to point to the oldest, best-dressed gentleman at the table to nominate him.

I thought, *you know what, I'm going to give this a try.*

Even though I was nervous, and felt a little like an imposter, I raised my hand and said, "I'd like to be the leader." They all shrugged and said "Okay, sure," and I led our table through the exercises. I have no idea whether I was the best leader at that table or not. It didn't matter. I stepped up. And guess who, out of all those people at that table, got to improve their leadership skills the most during that time? Me. Because I raised my hand.

While I've listed this as the third self-limiting belief in this chapter, this is the core belief that all others stem from. However, it's so prevalent that sometimes it shows up unfiltered on its own, without trying to disguise itself.

Exploration

To get to the bottom of any beliefs around a lack of worthiness, here are some additional questions:

- Do you downplay your achievements? If so, what awareness do you have about why?
- Do you feel guilty when you tell people about your accomplishments?
- Do you ever feel that you're a fraud and worry that someone might find out?
- When things are going well, what fears come up?
- When someone compliments or thanks you, do you say (or believe) "That's no big deal" or "Oh, it wasn't because of me" and so on? What is your inner dialog?

For each question you answered "Yes" to, take some time to explore that. What could be the sources of that belief? How is it holding you back? If that's an untrue belief, what's the truth?

As you go through the other beliefs, keep this one in mind and see if you can see how they relate.

Perfection = Success

The perfectionism curse. That insane drive to do everything perfectly. Many people chuckle when they read the first sentence because they see this self-limiting belief so clearly in their own life.

Keep in mind that the drive to be perfect can be helpful when deployed at the right times, in the right way (like all these other ways of behaving). It's only when perfectionism drives us, rather than us choosing it, that we run into issues. After all, as one of my teachers said once, "Perfectionism is a socially acceptable form of self-abuse." Left unchecked, it will stress you out, make you insane, and drive others away.

There are two ways in which this belief shows up. The first is commonly understood: it shows up in the incessant drive to be perfect. You're likely familiar enough with this self-limiting behavior and it's well worth releasing it.

The other way in which perfectionism shows up, and can be hard to grasp, is when you *are already* successful, but you make a subconscious agreement with yourself that you must do everything in your life *perfectly*. It's like you constantly have to *earn* your success through perfection. This variation can be harder to identify, but once I learned about it myself, I knew that this belief had a firm hold on me, and that it was causing me major angst.

When things were going well, I was determined to have everything in my life work out in perfect order. That would cause me to stress out over things I normally wouldn't take so seriously. I noticed that when I was doing well at work, I would get fanatical, expecting that everything in my life should go as planned—a sales presentation, preparing a proposal, cooking dinner, whatever.

Look carefully at your behaviors to pinpoint where either type of perfectionism shows up. It could be in your appearance, how you speak, how you write, your projects, what you expect from others, or any other aspect of your life.

Exploration

Here are some supporting questions to help you identify this belief:

- Are you never satisfied? Explore why if so.
- Do you dwell on the one thing you didn't do perfectly—even when you've had success—versus all the things you did get right?
- Do small tasks give you as much as, or more anxiety as large ones? Do you feel every job has to be done perfectly, no matter its size?

- Are you happy and content? What needs to be in place for that to be true?
- When someone praises you, do you say or believe: "Yes, but…"?

For each question you answered "Yes" to, take some time to explore that. What could be the sources of that belief? How is it holding you back? If that's an untrue belief, what's the truth?

Leaders, in particular, have to make so many decisions with limited information that trying to be perfect can hold them back, and the impact on their teams can create big challenges. Take a good look at these questions to see how much this one impacts you.

The Lone Wolf

Almost all self-made entrepreneurs share this particular belief. I see it frequently in my clients. It sounds like this:

"I need to do things on my own."

"I know better."

"Other people will just mess things up."

"Even if I succeed as part of a team, it won't mean as much as if I succeed on my own."

I used to have this belief—big time. Now I'm (mostly) over it…

I was driven to do everything by myself and didn't count any victories that weren't mine alone. For example, if you and I partnered to make a million dollars in a month, I wouldn't see it as a total victory because I didn't do it all myself.

Trying to do everything yourself is a difficult way to go through life, and especially as a leader, you'll never come close to realizing your full potential until you let go of this belief and start letting other people in.

You've probably had success in small areas working exactly your way. Because you're smart, can quickly pick up almost anything, and work with intense focus, at the end of the day you'll find a way to succeed. The problem is that you need to scale your team and your thinking to get to the next level *without killing yourself*. And you can't do that with this self-limiting belief in place.

Even when you try to work with others, you probably get frustrated easily, because you don't perceive them to be as smart or as dedicated as you, or they don't think the same way you do. So rather than spending time bringing them up to speed, you convince yourself it's easier and more efficient to get rid of them and do it solo.

When you're a lone wolf like this, you may not realize it, but it's easy to burn bridges. When you get defensive about your independent streak, and exclude or cut other people off, you miss any chance of connection with them. Anything that they were going to bring to the table—new ideas, new opportunities, new relationships—all vanish along with them. In short order, they grow to distrust and, frankly, dislike you. This is one of the reasons why people who are overly independent often have trouble connecting and having close, intimate relationships with others.

Your independence, drive and resilience are gifts. They have no doubt served you well at many times in your life. But if what you're reading here resonates with you, you're overusing them. Your need to be independent is holding you back personally and professionally, keeping you from the truth that the world is full of new ideas and possibilities that often come to us through other people.

Not only that, but if you're trying to do every job that needs to be done because you can't trust anyone else to do it, you're missing out on life. You can't get it all done yourself while learning and growing, much less enjoy yourself. You're stuck in the tactical when you need to be strategic, because strategic leaders let go and delegate.

If you want to be a strategic leader, you have to empower others. How are you going to scale up your business if you're the only expert in everything? If anything, that attitude is a surefire way to hold yourself back—you'll only grow as big as your own skill set and limited time will allow. Instead, find people and firms that know how to do their job better than you. Lead them, or accept their input and move forward. Don't try to reinvent the wheel over and over.

And keep in mind that people don't expect leaders to know or do it all. What they do expect is that their leader can show them the way to the solution.

Exploration

Do any of the following sound familiar?

- Do you resist asking for help?
- Do you work hard to not show any weaknesses?
- Do you have a burning desire to work on your own terms, even to the point where you reject input from experts or other authorities?
- If you accomplished something with someone else, would that diminish the value of the result in your eyes?
- Do you have issues delegating? Do you make everything run through you because you don't trust others to make the right decisions?
- Are you the person who always takes the other side of an argument because you always know a better way?

For each question you answered "Yes" to, take some time to explore. What could be the sources of that belief? How is it holding you back? If that's an untrue belief, what's the truth?

As painful as it may be to look in the mirror on this one, the payoff is big. It's the last of the most common self-limiting beliefs that pertains to leaders like you, and I hope you'll give it—and all the others—the attention it deserves.

CHAPTER 9:

Free Yourself
With Affirmations

Now that you've learned many of the devious ways that your subconscious beliefs are holding you back, the big question remains: how do you clear and heal them?

Answering that question could be the subject of a whole set of books, however the quickest and easiest way to take a bite out of your self-limiting beliefs is to create what's called an affirmation. This is a technique that rewires the pathways in your brain for healthier, stronger behaviors. Affirmations are powerful, positive statements that counteract self-limiting beliefs.

They all start with the words *"I am"* as if the desired behavior is happening already. By saying "I am" you're also indicating what you want as a positive (versus what you don't want, in the negative). That's because the brain on that level only understands simple commands. If you told your brain "the cloud is not blue" it would perceive "the cloud is blue."

Affirmations should be powerful and stir some emotion within you. That emotion could be excitement, or even a little anxiety, as you know whatever you're saying is going to get you to a new level. However, if an affirmation brings up too much anxiety or stress, you should dial it back. You should feel that it's at least 50% believable.

Affirmations could sound like:

- I am working 40 hours or fewer per week and am exceptionally effective, continuing to grow at a rapid pace. (This affirmation overcomes the *Work = Success* belief.)
- I'm healthy and filled with energy, I have a very happy and strong family life, and my work is fun and successful. (This affirmation overcomes the *Success Trade-Offs* belief.)
- I am attaining great abundance as I know I'm worthy of this success. (This affirmation overcomes the *Lack of Worthiness* belief.)
- I am productive, and take risks, sometimes failing, often succeeding, always learning—knowing that I'm a great creator. (This overcomes the *Perfection = Success* belief.)
- I am open to listening and taking in other people's expertise, opinion, and advice, as I use every situation to learn, grow, and connect. (This overcomes the *Lone Wolf* belief.)

Exploration

Now it's your turn to write your affirmations. They can be from the list above, adaptations, or entirely different. Say them out loud every day until you *feel* them taking hold in your body. You'll know when you've said them enough as you'll feel a shift internally. Some days, you'll only have to repeat the statements once or twice. On other days, more.

Some people tape their affirmations to their mirror and say them when they brush their teeth. Others tape them to their steering wheel. Some have them as their screen saver or password. An advanced approach to affirmations is to face a mirror, look into your own eyes, and then repeat the affirmation.

A few small tips to keep in mind:

- Say them out loud with confidence—even if you have some doubts. (ESPECIALLY if you have some doubts.)
- A great time to say your affirmations is after meditation, when your brain is in a relaxed state. Refer back to the mindfulness chapter for guidance on a simple meditation.
- You can have one affirmation or several, but refrain from too many. I personally find that any more than three, and they start to lose their effectiveness.
- You can change, upgrade, or eliminate your affirmations at any time. If a few days go by and one of yours loses its charge, consider whether it's run its course. Some affirmations are good for a few weeks; others for the rest of your life.
- You may use an affirmation to get through a potentially difficult or stressful time, for example: "I am calm and rational as I successfully sell my business for more than xxx dollars."

Affirmations are particularly useful because they're so straightforward to do. I frequently run leaders through the affirmations exercise in retreats and masterminds. Often, I'll see someone months or years after they went through the process, and they tell me, "I still say my affirmation every day."

You've just done some heavy lifting through identifying and clearing these subconscious self-limiting beliefs. The rest of this section will highlight some additional blindspots that leaders can release in order to evolve.

CHAPTER 10:

The Experienced Leader's Mask

Let's continue to identify what blocks many leaders and answer the question, "Why are you where you are, and not where you want to be?" No matter what size or type of organization you're in, you may have what I call the Experienced Leader, or Senior Manager's Mask.

When I meet senior-level executives and I ask them how things are going—even in a private, confidential setting like an initial coaching session—a vast majority of them respond, "It's all going pretty well."

As I probe more deeply, they try to justify their initial answer, but there's only so long they can hold up the facade. By the time the session is over, it's revealed that they're drinking themselves to sleep every night, their wife's about to leave them, they have no relationship with their kids, and they absolutely hate work.

People who reach a higher level in an organization, or scale a business for a number of years, can be in denial about their discontent. They're stuck in their ego pretending to be "pretty good" because they've been living in that zone for years. This is even more common in larger corporations where there's pressure to fit in. In many of these environments there's an inherent competitiveness that puts pressure on anyone who shows weakness, doesn't conform, gets caught on the wrong side of office politics, takes a big risk, or misses a yearly target.

Conformity isn't uniformly bad. Neither are goals. And politics are a natural part of any group—though like anything else they can be used in a positive, authentic way, or against the greater good. But senior leaders are under so much pressure to perform, and have such a desire to fit in and succeed, that they will build up an identity that they want people to see—and more importantly, an identity they want to fit into.

These people are extremely smart, driven, and headstrong, but unfortunately, in this area of their lives, these characteristics work against them. They've been subconsciously operating from their ego—in a mode of succeeding through fitting in and being accepted—for such a long time that it's become part of their identity.

What I've observed is that their life is a race to accumulate money, status, and power, and even though it's not bringing them any satisfaction, they're scared to death to even consider changing their approach. That's why they have such a strong defense mechanism—because if they're honest, the whole world and life they've spent so many years building, isn't what they want.

It doesn't happen easily, but when the experienced leader finally lets their guard down, there's usually a lot they've compartmentalized and repressed. It is, however, a thing of beauty when they find the time and will to address these behaviors head-on and work to free themselves.

This doesn't happen only with corporate employees. Business owners also have to keep evaluating in order to make sure they're evolving—themselves, their role, and their skillset.

For example, an experienced business owner named Tim once saw me speak at an event and got in touch after the presentation. He told me that his company had been growing, but that had leveled off and he didn't know how to get back on the path to scaling his business. After hearing me talk about leadership mindset, he told me, "That was the light bulb moment where I realized something was broken. To get to our goals something had to change, and that something was me."

Through deep inner work and reflection, it came out that his ego loved the times that he swooped in at the last minute and solved the problem or closed the latest big sale. He had been in denial about this for years. He was actually addicted to the dopamine hit this would produce, so he would subconsciously set up ways to be the hero.

When Tim learned to slow down, listen, and start coaching and empowering others, his company transformed. He reported back that two employees said it was the best company they'd ever worked for. Furthermore, he started finding empowering others more fulfilling than being the hero ever did.

With all of your experience, are you in a state of denial about the status quo? Do you have areas in your life where you have serious discontent? Maybe you don't know what to do about it because you don't see a quick, easy fix, so you ignore it and hope it goes away.

It takes courage to be truly vulnerable; this doesn't mean telling a vulnerable story you've already thought of and practiced in order to seem vulnerable. It means taking ownership and admitting that you aren't perfect and you don't have everything handled—yet also having the resolve and focus to learn and adapt for your own growth.

As the saying goes, "Hope is not a strategy." When you stay in denial about your discontent, it impacts your energy and how you lead, whether you realize it or not.

Exploration

Take a few minutes to reflect on your life. How much do you like your job? How much do you like the company you're working for? How excited are you to get to work each morning? What's your general happiness level?

Now, think of someone you love. If you have a child, think of them, or anyone else you hold dear. Allow yourself to be moved by your love for them. Now, holding on to that feeling, visualize them standing in your shoes, inserted into your life, going through all of your experiences. Would you want your current level of happiness and satisfaction for the person you love? Are you happy with what this special person would experience if they took your spot in life?

If not, what would you tell them to do differently? And how does that help you see what to do differently for yourself?

CHAPTER 11:

The Entrepreneurial Curse

There's another common issue with people who have the courage and willpower to start their own business, or, who have the entrepreneurial spirit within a larger company, sometimes called being intrapreneurial. People like this always want to do things themselves, their own way—even when it's to their own detriment.

As you know, it takes immense willpower and energy to risk starting your own business, lead a new department, or spearhead a ground-breaking initiative. Often, you have to shake off the opinions of your family, friends, and even industry experts. Over time, you learn to shut everyone else off and only listen to yourself. After all, it's that supreme self-belief that's carried you to this point.

Having been in your shoes, I understand how easily it can start to feel like you can't trust anyone but yourself, and to live the saying, "If you want something done right, do it yourself." This mentality, however, also means that entrepreneurial types tend not to delegate, rarely open up to others, and resist being coached. (They are actually famous within the coaching profession for being hard to coach.)

The difficult skill to master here is discerning when to follow your own conviction and when to give in and trust someone else. Because the larger your company gets, the more success you create, and the more you'll need to rely on others.

At some point, as a leader in business, you simply DO NOT "know better." There are a lot of best practices you can learn that will make things much easier and give you a solid platform to grow and scale. Do you really think you can scale if the company is relying on you to oversee marketing and handle sales? Or if you get involved with product development like you have been?

The added difficulty is that in the past, you may have tried to off-load projects or responsibilities to others before, or even brought in subject matter experts, and failed, making you gun-shy to do it again. This can lead to an incredible amount of over-control, and an overdeveloped sense of responsibility. Ultimately this becomes a severe bottleneck to growth—not to mention a recipe for burnout.

Once you've learned to trust, work with others, and *lead* them, you won't have to babysit these growth areas. Others have done it; you can too. After all, it's not like you're the only one in the world wired this way.

I can spot people who are in denial about this because when I speak or teach, they're the ones who'll come up and tell me how much of what I'm teaching they already know, or they're already doing. If that's you, here's my challenge to you:

As you read things in these pages that you feel familiar with, ask, "*Where aren't I doing this?*" or "*How can I do that to a deeper level?*" The leadership tools and skills you're learning here are not things you'll ever master—there will always be new opportunities to apply them, whether that's to different relationships, situations, or conversations. When you ask the deeper questions, you'll find answers that change the way you see the world.

Exploration

Reminder: as you read this book, or learn anything, for that matter, don't get caught in the "validation" trap. This is what happens when you read something you've heard before, you think *I know that already,* and then place it aside.

The Buddhists have a concept called "beginners mind" where you approach anything you run across as if it's the first time. That way you won't be distracted by assumptions and preconceived notions.

CHAPTER 12:

Releasing Judgments

In addition to self-limiting beliefs, there are a few more important impediments to release before we move onto rewiring our minds. One of these is judgments. While I had heard the term judgment a lot in my life, I never knew what it exactly meant. When I learned the definition, and how it affects our inner life, it changed how I saw the world.

To learn more about judgments and land on a definition we can use as leaders, let's first look at the Buddhist virtue called *upekkha*. American Buddhist monk Bhikkhu Bodhi wrote [15]:

> "The real meaning of upekkha is equanimity, not indifference in the sense of unconcern for others. As a spiritual virtue, upekkha means stability in the face of the fluctuations of worldly fortune. It is evenness of mind, unshakeable freedom of mind, a state of inner equipoise that cannot be upset by gain and loss, honor and dishonor, praise and blame, pleasure and pain.
>
> Upekkha is freedom from all points of self-reference; it is indifference only to the demands of the ego-self with its

---

15   Bodhi, Bhikkhu (5 June 2010) [1998]. "Toward a Threshold of Understanding". Access to Insight. Barre Center for Buddhist Studies. Retrieved 2013-10-07

craving for pleasure and position, not to the well-being of one's fellow human beings.

True equanimity is the pinnacle of the four social attitudes that the Buddhist texts call the 'divine abodes': boundless loving-kindness, compassion, altruistic joy, and equanimity. The last does not override and negate the preceding three, but perfects and consummates them."

To break this all down, a judgment, in my simple definition for leaders, is simply *a meaning the ego attaches to something.*

Buddhists say that when something happens, there's only one truth: that it happened. Or you can say "*it is.*" But what most of us do as humans is attach a *good* or *bad* meaning to it. That's the judgment (see Figure 11: Judgments.)

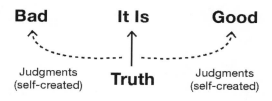

Figure 11: Judgments

In fact, many religions echo this. Catholics say *"Do not judge, and you will not be judged. Do not condemn, and you will not be condemned. Forgive, and you will be forgiven."* [Luke 6:37] The Jewish scholar Rabbi Hillel wrote *"Don't judge your fellow human being until you have reached that person's place."* And in Islam, it's written that *"O you who have faith! Avoid much suspicion. Indeed, some suspicions are sins."* [Surah Hujurat:12]

Even the ancient Greek philosopher Plato said "I have this tattooed on my left side! I love the saying and it's a perfect description of

Karma: *Don't judge, discriminate or do to someone what you wouldn't want done to you."*

If Plato had that tattooed on his left side, we better dig deeper into it...

Here's an example that illustrates judgment. Say I was dating a woman and she broke up with me. The truth is that it happened. It is. As a human, I may assign a negative to that situation. *"Oh no, I'm not attractive, I'll never get married. I'm a loser."* Or I could assign a positive to it. *"She wasn't the right person for me anyway." "Now I'm free to find the right person."*

Both of those are meanings I could choose to attach to what happened. Neither is necessarily true; they're how I choose to look at the situation. The only truth here, again, is that she broke up with me. It's a neutral fact. The opposite of judging is acceptance. You move into acceptance by dealing with the neutral facts without adding meaning to the truth.

How does this affect us in everyday life, and in leadership in particular? Here's how I shifted from judgment to acceptance, and it also shows the change in my everyday life.

I used to be a bit of a "drama queen." I come from a family where passing judgment was normal and natural. Everything that came in during my workday, I would assign a positive or negative value. After talking to a prospective client, I would get really high and say, "I had this great call and we're gonna make so much money off this client!"

The next minute somebody would come in and inform me that they'd be on holiday all next week, and I'd start worrying about how hard it would be without them around. I was like this literally every hour, almost minute to minute; I was on this up and down roller coaster (Figure 12: The Roller Coaster of Judgments2). By the end of the day, my energy levels were totally depleted. I was drained and exhausted.

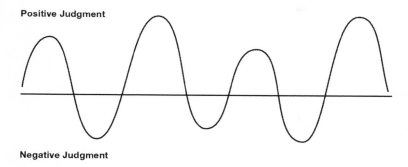

Figure 12: The Roller Coaster of Judgments

My inner chatter would go from "*That sucks!*" in one moment to "*This is amazing!*" in the next. Whatever came across my field of view got a positive or negative attached to it, and I would often voice those judgments to whoever was around me.

When I learned about judging and accepting, the distinction hit home. I hadn't known that judging was an unproductive thing to do; it just felt like a natural reaction for me. After realizing the impact of my judging, I decided to release it and committed to changing.

For three months, I put a lot of intention and focus into moving from judgment to acceptance—dealing with the neutral facts without adding meaning to the truth. It wasn't easy, and it took a few weeks before I started to get it. But slowly, with daily work, I did. And it made a huge difference.

Of course, I still had emotional reactions—I'm not a robot after all. And some emotions are natural and healthy, even ones like frustration. But the negative emotions were a fraction of what they'd been before and they were much less dramatic. By smoothing out the massive emotional ups and downs I was used to, I found that by the end of the day I had much more energy remaining (Figure 13).

Positive Judgment

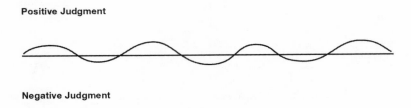

Negative Judgment

Figure 13: The Smoothness of Acceptance

My decision-making also improved significantly because I wasn't making decisions based on emotion. Think back for a moment to the worst choices you've made in your life. Chances are they were made when you were in a highly emotional state, either a very high emotion such as extreme happiness, when you're overly optimistic, or a very low emotion like sadness, anger or frustration.

When I released judgement, and moved into a state of acceptance, I saw situations for what they were—information. Data. Pieces of the puzzle to make the next decision with. This is not to say that we should operate as computers; what you need to learn is to make decisions from a calm, level-headed state of mind.

Another major benefit of this change is that I became the calm, patient leader who was the voice of reason for others and could be counted on to have the right answer in chaotic times. People would come to me in an emotional state, and my evenness would calm them down. Then together, we would create a well-thought out way forward. Isn't that the type of leader people love to follow, and isn't that the type of leader you want to be?

Moving from judging to accepting is one of the most powerful shifts you can make, and to assist in that, let me clear up some common misconceptions:

Misconception 1: Evaluating vs. Judging

First, there's a difference between evaluating and judging. You can absolutely evaluate something without placing judgment on its meaning.

"I do not like mint chocolate chip ice cream" is an evaluation. It's not a judgment. You're not saying mint chocolate chip ice cream is bad, only that you don't enjoy it personally.

You might say, "That person's acting like a jerk." How you say it—the intention behind it—differentiates whether it's an evaluation or judgment. If it's said with anger and malice, it's a judgment. However, it could also be a true statement that they are objectively acting like a jerk. It is possible—and even necessary—to evaluate things in life.

That person isn't trustworthy.

He isn't very helpful.

She's late a lot.

They aren't very good at their job.

These can all be evaluations if they're said without blame or anger.

Misconception 2: Agreeing and Judging

The second misconception is that there's a difference between agreeing and judging. It's possible to not agree with something and still accept it.

Let's imagine that I'm out in the world, and I get pickpocketed. I can accept the fact that this happened to me and I can still report it to the police. I can live with the fact that I was robbed and still hope I get my wallet back. I can understand that people sometimes get pickpocketed in the world and still hope the person gets caught and punished. I can accept all of these things, however I don't have to agree with stealing. I can follow the system by reporting the theft, and have the police handle it. But that doesn't mean I have to lose my power and get upset over it. I can go through that whole process without ever getting angry.

When you watch the news, for example, it's possible to not agree with something that's happening or that someone says. You don't have to get upset or angry; you can still keep your calm and peace about you.

Misconception 3: Positive and Negative Judgments

The third of our misconceptions about judgments is that we're not too concerned with "positive" judgments. If you label something as "good" that's normally not an issue—unless you get so caught up in the positive judgment that you aren't seeing things rationally.

To make change in your life, become aware of your negative judgments and focus on letting go of them. For example, I found that if I didn't like a politician, I thought that every single decision they made was bad. After I realized this belief, I tested it. There was a politician who I didn't like or respect. As I paid more attention, this person made some moves that I actually supported. From then on, I made the decision that I would withhold my judgment of the person and decide on a case-by-case basis which decisions I supported or opposed.

Keep this in mind as you consider the state of the world. By almost every meaningful measure [16], life today globally is better than it ever has been. Worldwide, malnutrition and extreme poverty are at historic lows, and the risk of dying by war or violence is the lowest in human history. In the United States, disease, discrimination, crime, and most forms of pollution are in decline over

---

16   For more information, see the book *It's Better Than It Looks: Reasons for Optimism in an Age of Fear* by Gregg Easterbrook

the long-term, while how long we live and the education levels we achieve keep rising. Economic indicators are better than in any past generation.

Does this mean that global warming doesn't exist? Of course not. Does this mean that we should keep helping the planet? Of course we should. However, to be strategic, we have to take things in context. We should still work to become greener, have fewer (or no!) wars, and help the disadvantaged. Let's do it with positive energy instead of hatred and anger, which is not a good way to go through life for anyone.

We're always going to make judgments; eliminating them completely is not a realistic goal. But—as we do in the trainings my company offers—we can train ourselves to make fewer judgments, and conserve a lot of energy to create results. We also can learn to catch ourselves in the moment and let judgments go swiftly so they don't fester.

Exploration

If you judged less, and accepted more, what would that mean for your life?

What do you judge? What is "bad" in your life? Who is "bad"?

How are your judgments affecting how people see you, your decision making, and your overall consciousness?

CHAPTER 13:

Forgiving Others

Remember the story I told you about my former business part-ner who assaulted me, which spiraled into a huge, horrible lawsuit? Here's what happened next.

After he got served with a restraining order, termination letter, and lawsuit, he found a new partner and started a competing company. He proceeded to call my existing clients to entice them to work with him, and also started recruiting my employees. I'd been angry at him already, but between the lawsuit and competing over clients and talent, we hated each other.

When we met to mediate the lawsuit, he told the whole room, in-cluding the meditator and both of our attorneys, that he despised me and would never settle the lawsuit. He wanted to see me burn. A few months later, he ran out of money, and we did settle, but not without a lot of stress.

My thoughts were consumed by him and his actions and I was constantly angry. *How dare he do this to me, then steal what I worked so hard to create? How could he be so brash to think I'm in the wrong?*

When an email came in from my attorney about the case, as soon as I saw the subject line, my whole body would tense up. I even had bad dreams about him. Just the mention of his name would set me off. I even remember bumping into a friend and her dog.

When I asked what the dog's name was, she told me, and it was the same name as my ex-business partner. My response was, "I hate your dog."

I was going through this difficult time in my life at the same time I started the Spiritual Psychology course. There, we learned about the concept of forgiveness and how, when we choose to hold onto a grievance, it only creates angst within ourselves.

Do you know what the antonym, or opposite, of forgiveness is? Punishment.

After the professor explained the overall concept of forgiveness, we broke up into pairs to work on an exercise based on our real-life experiences. The woman I was partners with asked, "Mike, who do you not get along with right now? Who do you hate?"

My first response was, "No one. I'm pretty happy and good with everyone in my life."

She gave me a look and asked again, "No, seriously. Who do you hate?"

"OK," I confessed. "I hate my business partner." And I proceeded to tell her some of the background. Listening carefully, she said, "Got it. Let me ask you this. When you hate him like this, how does it affect his life?"

I was confused. "What do you mean?"

"How is his life different whether you hate him or not?" she asked.

This question stopped me in my tracks. "Well...it's not," I replied.

That's when I got it. When we hate someone like I hated my business partner, the only person impacted was me. His life didn't change one iota. It was only bringing *me* down. I sat there pondering this when, after a minute, my partner said, "Can I ask you another question?"

"Yes," I said, as I refocused on her.

"If the situation were reversed and you were kicked out of a company that you helped build—granted you may not have assaulted anyone—but say you felt wronged, what would you do?"

It didn't take long for the answer to come to my mind. "Well…I probably would have created a competing company and stolen his clients and employees, the same as what he's doing to me."

That little bit of compassion for him helped me see everything in a new light.

Then she asked, "Can you forgive him? Forgive your business partner?"

I sighed and let everything settle in for a moment before answering. "Yes. I forgive him."

As I said those three small words, it felt like a weight was lifted off my shoulders. Just having the intention and saying I forgave him was all it took for my state to change from victim to owner.

When I tell this story, people often ask me, "But did you really forgive him—completely?" The answer is no. Yes, I forgave him, but it's true that I didn't let all of it go in that exact second. In fact, I'd say I still have a tiny bit of resentment, and maybe always will. But I can tell you that forgiving someone 80%, 40%, or even 1% is a lot better than not at all. A lot better.

Other people ask, "Have you talked to your business partner to clear the air?" Again, the answer is no. Part of me would like to sit down with him and do just that. But the situation hasn't presented itself, and of course, I don't know if he'd be receptive.

The point is that forgiving someone doesn't have anything to do with them. It's strictly your choice and your decision. They're not actually involved.

Taking this one step further, you may be familiar with the concept that *everyone's doing the best they can, given their current circumstances, and their current knowledge.* This means that on some level, every action and decision someone makes is because some part of them thinks it's the right thing to do.

For you as a leader, that means that when someone does something that's incorrect, it's up to you to figure out WHY they did it. Very few people, outside of those working in a openly hostile and toxic culture, will ever mess up on purpose. Something prompted them to do things that way.

Maybe they thought they were doing it correctly. Maybe they had a self-limiting belief. Maybe they got confused or the instructions were wrong. Maybe they don't have the skills or mindset for the job. Maybe they were overloaded.

All of the above reasons are opportunities for you to work with them and coach them on solutions. Doing that will build trust, loyalty, and connection, and turn a potentially disruptive issue into a learning opportunity.

Exploration

Who are you upset with and in a nutshell, why?

Now, remind yourself that in the upset scenario you've identified, you're 100% responsible for your internal state of mind. Also remember that whoever you're upset with is another human being, and they had a reason—maybe even a good one—for doing what they did. It's up to you how you hold that inside yourself.

Finally, go ahead and simply tell yourself, internally or out loud, that you forgive them. Say it a few times, possibly with your eyes closed—concentrate on letting the emotion go each time you say it. Even if you release only 1% of what you're holding onto, you've made progress.

CHAPTER 14:

Self-Forgiveness

There's just one more part to the process I was going through with the woman at my school. Her next question was, "Do you judge yourself for bringing him in as a business partner?"

"Yes," I answered right away. "I screwed up for giving him that equity. I caused all this. I should have known better and handled everything differently."

She then asked, "When you met him, why did you make him your business partner?"

"We were growing fast, he was dedicated and giving a lot to the firm, and doing well. But there were some signs—clues that this would happen. I'm so stupid for not seeing them."

"Sounds like you were under a lot of stress, and as I recall, this was the first time you were in that situation—it was your first business, is that right?"

"Yes that's all correct."

"It also sounds like he did contribute to growing the business for a few years."

"Yes, also correct."

"And did you learn a lot about leadership and people through this situation?"

"I sure did. I learned about that, a lot more to do with legal agreements, the legal process, partnerships, and many other things."

"When you think back to yourself a few years ago when you made the decision to bring him on, can you see that you were making the best decision you could at the time? Can you give yourself a break, cut yourself some slack?"

Wow. I thought about all she was asking. I had been young and inexperienced and I'd had to make so many decisions so quickly. In certain ways, things did work out. And who was to know it would end up like this?

"Yes," I answered, "yes, I can cut myself some slack."

Like any great coach, she made sure to bring the learning home. "So Mike, do you forgive yourself for bringing on your business partner? Can you come into love and compassion with yourself?"

I sighed again. My inner voice was angry at me for making that decision and would constantly tell me how stupid it was. And now I was being asked to accept that, and myself? I figured I would give it a try.

"I forgive myself for making that decision. I was doing the best I could at the time. And I gained a lot out of it."

As I said the words, something else inside me shifted. I again felt lighter, but in a different way. In a way that made me feel more at peace. This was self-forgiveness.

In my Master's program, we spent a whole year—50% of the whole degree—on self-forgiveness. We looked at it from every different angle and gained mastery of it. At the end of the day, the relationship that trumps all others is the relationship you have with yourself. Your relationship with everything else—your team, your board, even your investors and your family—is a projection of the relationship you have with yourself.

Through the work you're doing right now, you're entering a stronger, more compassionate, loving relationship with yourself. A lot of that journey is done by identifying and changing your ego-based inner chatter, which comes from judgments you have against yourself, most of which were originally brought on by self-limiting beliefs.

By the way, forgiveness, self-limiting beliefs, and all that we're covering in Leadership Mindset 2.0 are advanced principles. Even if they don't totally click now, that's OK. Think of them as seeds that will take time to grow. It took me months to start to integrate these things properly.

The next time you try self-forgiveness for something you've done as a leader, there's a subtle detail to keep in mind. You're not forgiving yourself for your actions—the things you did. You're forgiving yourself for the judgments you have around doing those actions. Come into acceptance for the action and release yourself from the judgment.

In my case, I needed to accept I was doing the best I could when I brought on my business partner. I needed to forgive all the judgments I had: judging that I was stupid, and judging that I should have known better.

Now, think about how this relates to leadership in the bigger picture. Leaders need resilience. We take on huge amounts of responsibility, make difficult decision after difficult decision, and manage constant change. You're going to make mistakes. When you can forgive yourself, you're no longer stuck in the past, second-guessing yourself or analyzing everything over and over again. You brush off the setback and get ready for what's next, back in the present and leading with power and confidence once again.

This doesn't mean you gloss over or minimize when things go wrong. We're talking about the ability to take full ownership of something but not let the setback define you. After all, Michael Jordan, possibly the greatest basketball player and crunch time performer ever, famously said, "I've missed more than 9,000 shots in my career. I've lost almost 300 games. Twenty-six times I've been trusted to take the game-winning shot and missed. I've failed over and over and over again in my life. And that is why I succeed."

I've screwed up a lot, too, and apologized many times. And I'm fine with all of it, because I'm human and I take a lot of risks. I'm not going to be perfect and the same goes for you. If you keep pushing yourself, leading people, and breaking through barriers, you're going to screw up too. It's natural, so give yourself a break and quit being so hard on yourself. Forgive yourself and let it all go so you have the energy, focus, and self-esteem to be the leader your team needs.

Also, keep an eye on your employees, ESPECIALLY your high performers. Sometimes they can drive themselves too hard, and look to you for validation for pushing that much. Help THEM with this as well. Build them up. Praise them, but be sincere with it. Don't get caught in the leadership trap of preying on their insecurities so they'll work harder and longer. You'll end up with a team of exhausted people, none of whom have the confidence in themselves to show any leadership, and you'll get stuck yourself.

By helping your high-performers develop their sense of self-esteem, like you're learning to do for yourself, you're developing future leaders who will be loyal and look up to you for the rest of their lives.

Exploration

What are you judging yourself for? What does your inner critic say you should've done differently? What are you down on yourself for? Really listen to that voice and what it says, making sure you hear and understand it. Take some time to feel the emotion around it as well, because the better you connect to those feelings, the more of it you can release when you're ready to forgive.

Remind yourself that you were doing the absolute best you knew to do given the information you had at the time. You're always evolving, and you can look at that particular time in the past as a learning experience. Whatever it is you're judging yourself for, you're still a worthy person. Learning to accept and love your whole self—imperfections and all—is significant.

Finally, to complete the integration process for now, say "I forgive myself for judging myself as _____." and fill in the blank with the negative comments you had towards yourself. Concentrate on feeling the release. Repeat this a few times, each time going deeper until you can feel things shift. Take note of how the shift feels.

Self-forgiveness is a crucial and powerful way to improve your relationship with yourself, and reaching your full potential.

The Growth Leadership Path

Phase 2:
Rewire and Reprogram

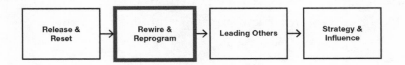

If you think of yourself as a glass you want to fill with the best leadership knowledge and mindset, you just took an important step in the previous chapters by first emptying the glass. With the thoughts and beliefs that were holding you back released, now it's time to fill you up with the thoughts and (true) beliefs that will enable you to reach your potential.

When I started on my growth path, I soon realized how much I was subconsciously holding myself back. After a lot of releasing and relearning, I started to live more and more in my authentic self. The result was that I created deeper bonds with people, the world slowed down and made more sense, and I was more at peace personally.

From there, I knew I needed to take the next step with my mindset to become a strong leader, the one my company needed me to be, and had been waiting for. The problem was I didn't know what that looked like. That's when I hired coaches and mentors, took trainings, read books, and surrounded myself with successful businesspeople, and it all resulted in what you're reading here, Leadership Mindset 2.0.

What you'll learn in the next section is the mindset you need to adopt in order to show up with powerful leadership presence, to develop unshakeable resilience, and to cultivate empathy and connections. These are the things that will cause people to trust and follow you through the highest of highs and lowest of lows.

Since your leadership is an extension of your relationship with yourself, that's what we'll be focusing on: intentionally developing that strong sense of self-esteem and confidence, and bringing out all of your best qualities to reach your full potential as a leader.

CHAPTER 15:

The Psychology of Imposter Syndrome

Imposter syndrome is *the persistent inability to believe that one's success is deserved or has been legitimately achieved as a result of one's own efforts or skills.*[17] *Think of it as perceived fraudulence, characterized by feelings of internal self-doubt in spite of external signals of success such as education, status, or a prominent career.* Basically, it means you feel like you don't belong, you doubt yourself and your capabilities, and you get scared other people will find out you're faking it.

Fact: Imposter Syndrome is extremely common—especially among high achievers. Up to 82%[18] of people experience it.

If you're reading this thinking, *I may feel like a fraud and imposter now, but once I start earning a certain amount of money, build my business to a certain level, or reach a certain position, I'm sure I'll outgrow it*…consider this short story first.

---

17   Oxford Language Dictionary

18   Bravata, D. M., Madhusudhan, D. K., Boroff, M., & Cokley, K. O. (2020). Commentary: Prevalence, predictors, and treatment of Imposter Syndrome: A systematic review. Journal of Mental Health & Clinical Psychology. https://www.mentalhealthjournal.org/articles/commentary-prevalence-predictors-and-treatment-of-imposter-syndrome-a-systematic-review.html

Some time ago, a Young President's Organization (YPO) forum brought me in for a day to work with them. This was a group of eight business owners, two of whom ran businesses with revenues over $2 billion a year.

After getting to know them, and reaching a place of pure honesty, *every single one of them admitted they feel like an imposter* in some (or many) areas of their lives. They felt like their businesses and lives were out of control; they were chasing fulfillment, peace, and true happiness but didn't seem to be getting any closer.

Imposter syndrome is simply your ego trying to protect you.

What happens when imposter syndrome strikes is a combination of brain science—the ego perceives a threat and doesn't want to give up control, feel uncomfortable, or allow you to lose your place in the group—and self-limiting beliefs, or psychological programming.

When you're experiencing imposter syndrome, first stop judging, and congratulate yourself. Most likely, you're experiencing this because you've worked hard—and smart—to build a company, get promoted into a position, or been handed responsibility that's new to you, and that's all because you've been doing things right. In this case, your imposter syndrome is a symptom of your success.

Even if that's NOT the case—maybe you fell into an opportunity, or don't feel like you've earned or deserved it—work on letting go of the judgment you have about feeling like an imposter. We're going to give you the tools and skills needed to overcome this so you can thrive.

I sure as heck have had imposter syndrome many times in the past. I still experience it today, mostly when I challenge and push myself. The difference now is that I can spot it, I know why it's there, and I know how to work with it to immediately shift it from something that holds me back to something that supports me.

What you'll learn now are the ways your ego tries to protect you by bringing up these feelings. In the following chapter, we'll go over tools and techniques to rewire yourself for confidence and success.

The Comparison Trap

Have you noted how often you compare yourself to others? How much money they make, what are they're wearing, what car they drive, even how their spouse/partner/kids stack up to yours?

That's what the ego does—it compares, finds differences and brings them to your attention.

Some people will advise you to stop comparing yourself to people who have more, or seem better, than you. The logic suggests that you should compare yourself to someone who's not doing well, because that will help you feel less behind, and less like a fraud. While that may work to a point, you're still feeding your ego, just in a different way.

Instead, the next time you fall into the comparison trap, try changing your thought process to look for commonalities. By doing this, you'll bypass your ego and its attempts to keep you playing small.

Rather than *that person makes more money than me*, rewire with thoughts like these:

- *That person has a similar background to me.*
- *They really care about their customers, just like I do.*
- *Looks like they have the same drive and work ethic as I do.*

Notice how the statements above change the energy from one thing being better than the other, to putting similar things together. When you realize how much you have in common with someone who's successful, you'll realize you have the ability to be successful yourself.

> ### Exploration
>
> When you catch yourself comparing, remember it's the ego doing its best to keep you safe.
>
> Take a look and notice the similarities between you and whoever or whatever your ego was comparing you with.

Failing and Doomsday Scenarios

When you seize an opportunity to take on a significant new project or customer, or step into a new job, you may find yourself asking, *what if I mess it up?* The protective tone of that question gives you a hint as to what part of you is talking. That's right, it's your ego again. Bear in mind that your ego is always on the lookout for ways things can go wrong, so it can convince you not to try anything new. After all, anything new is a risk and our egos hate risk.

As you evolve in your leadership, you'll discover that your ego will attempt to link everything that could go wrong to a doomsday scenario that has almost no chance of happening.

Sometimes when my phone rings, thanks to my ego, my train of thought does the following:

Oh no, it's my largest customer calling to cancel their contract to...

Next all the other customers will find out and cancel theirs to...

I'm going to have to shut down the company to...

I'm going to be homeless.

That's exactly how it plays out. In a hundredth of a second, in my own mind I've become a fraud and an imposter with no right to be where I am. Then, I shake it off and answer the phone. Sometimes when I'm speaking or training, I'll mention this pattern and ask the audience whether they've experienced anything similar. Over half of the group raises their hands—every time. I've also noticed this internal dialog happening when I'm in great financial shape and life overall is going well. Perhaps you can guess why that is. My achievements are outpacing my self-worth, like we covered in an earlier chapter. An internal part of me doesn't feel worthy enough for my external success, so my ego starts playing games.

Exploration

The next time you have an opportunity in front of you and your ego is naming the reasons why you shouldn't go after it, write them all down. Use your rational mind to mark down which items are legitimate concerns and which are your ego trying to protect you. Then write down all the reasons it IS a good opportunity and absorb that list to counter the doomsday narrative and allow your imposter syndrome to fade.

An exercise like this is good to review with your coach or a trusted friend as it can be challenging to see past your ego and emotions, especially when there are big decisions on the horizon.

Perfectionism, Procrastination and Control

Here's another way imposter syndrome shows up. When we subconsciously aim for perfect, there's simply no way to achieve those expectations—therefore we must be a fraud.

To illustrate this, consider a job which lists five qualifications and a potential male candidate has two, he'll apply for the job. Yet if a potential female candidate has four of the qualifications, she won't apply because she doesn't have all five. While that's a generalization, it gets a lot of anecdotal support from women leaders who nod their heads in frustrated agreement. Their inner dialog, as directed by their ego, gives them the message: "I'm not perfect for the job so I'm not worthy of applying, so I won't bother."

Perfectionism leads directly to inaction. Feeling as if you don't have control of everything will also lead you to inaction. As usual, the ego wants to control everything and will resist taking action until it thinks it has everything under control. Don't let it win.

The fact is that life is risky, and if you want to grow, you'll need to get used to making decisions with incomplete information and no guarantee. It's OK to fail. It's fine to make changes after you've already started. It may be difficult, and the end result may not be what you had in mind at the start, but you'll get there. I've found that by sidestepping perfectionism, the outcome is even better than I imagined. Go for that next-level job. Open up the new location. Buy that business. Take your shot.

After all, when you read successful people's biographies, they're not littered with stories about not taking action when they didn't know what the outcome would be. The stories we hear are all about stepping up boldly, taking risks, testing themselves, and—most of the time—succeeding.

Exploration

What do you think about doing…but don't do? Where are you striving to be perfect, when you don't need to be?

Don't just consider your work life. Look at your personal life as well to see where this is showing up.

Talking Yourself Out of Action

Something else happens when we're in the grip of imposter syndrome, and that is talking ourselves out of things. How often does your inner voice convince you that you're not equipped to even try something? There are several common "inner voice" statements which are worth looking at in turn:

You should know how to do this already.

This statement implies that you shouldn't even try something unless you've been trained, certified, and have years of experience doing it. But that isn't logical—everyone's a beginner at some point. Your intelligence, drive to succeed, and ability to learn will overcome your lack of experience.

You should have all the answers.

Do you ever say no to a challenge because you're concerned someone will ask, "What will you do if this happens? Or that happens?" Yes, you may get asked that question. And a perfectly fine answer is, "I don't know."

My answer to what-if questions is, "I don't deal in hypothetical what-if's. When things come up, we'll handle them." What this voice is really wanting to hear is that you'll be on top of things. A little confidence and self-assurance go a long way, even if you have some doubts yourself.

You should be able to do things by yourself.

The fact that you don't know how to take on a task by yourself doesn't mean you shouldn't take it on. In this complex world, there's no shame in hiring someone, asking a colleague for help, getting a coach or mentor, or looking online.

As a leader, your job is not to *do* everything, it's to get a result. Often, that means bringing in the right person for the job. That's not a weakness—it's leadership.

Exploration

What expectations do you have for yourself regarding a current, potential or upcoming role, or strategic move in your business?

If you were to look at this scenario from the outside, and someone else was in your place, what expectations would you have of them? It's very likely you'd have less difficult and more realistic expectations, and overall more compassion. Keeping that in mind, adjust the expectations you have of yourself.

CHAPTER 16:

Overcoming Imposter Syndrome

Now that you understand that your ego is trying to protect you, and how that can keep you stuck in imposter syndrome, it's time to give you a toolkit for releasing its grip and unleashing your most powerful, authentic self. We're now ready for the practical aspect of rewiring and reprogramming.

One simple technique involves using logic to overcome your self-doubt. When you find yourself in a situation where you feel like a fraud and don't belong, you can ask your inner critic, *"Why not me? I've earned this, and I have a track record of success. Someone had enough faith to put me here, so I'm going to give it a try..."*

I recall a conversation I had with a business owner who overcame crippling imposter syndrome by telling himself, *"It doesn't matter why I'm here. The only time is now. Right now, I'm here in this situation, I'm fully present, and I'm going to do whatever I can in this moment to succeed."* That simple mantra shifted his mindset and was all he needed to lead his company to the next few levels of scaling and growth.

While that's more of a quick hack, what follows are several hands-on tools you can use to overcome your sense of imposter syndrome.

The 50 Stack Technique

Take a stack of 50 blank or lined notecards. On each one, write down 50 reasons why.

"Wait, why what, Mike?" Good question. The "why" depends on the intention of your 50 Stack. It should address where you're feeling doubt or out of place. Here are two examples:

- If you're going for a new job, write down 50 reasons why you're the right person for that job and will succeed.
- If you're scaling your company, write down 50 reasons why you have the ability to grow the company.

Fifty sounds like a lot—because it is. Most people take more than one brainstorming session to get to fifty. Don't forget to include past successes, your abilities, anything you can think of as evidence for "why."

Now, keep this 50 Stack close at hand. When you feel doubt making its way into your mindset, pick up your weighty stack of cards and read through some. Between the process of writing them down, which generates good energy to combat the sense of being a fraud, plus the act of reviewing, the 50 Stack Technique is a strong way to build confidence for your new initiatives.

The Brag Book

Over the years, I've noticed that leaders accomplish a lot of impressive things, including both personal and professional wins. They just hide them under a mountain of self-worth issues which make them invisible when they're really needed—in the present moment!

Get a notebook and a good pen[19] you enjoy writing with, and start writing down your accomplishments. They could be from any time

---

19   Side note: The Pentel Energel Retractable Gel Pen is my favorite - so much so that I get upset with my wife when she swipes them from my desk–which is more infuriating than you would think...

in your life, for example your childhood, your school years, or your recent career path. The accomplishments can be related to work, sport, family, or social. Note down anything you look back with fondness on, anything that resulted in a successful outcome—a big risk you took, a situation where you helped someone, something you've achieved notoriety for, even a moment of tenderness or vulnerability. If you're proud of it, it goes in the notebook.

Be thorough with the list and go back on different days, at least twice more, to add to it.

Once you're done, at least for the moment, step back and look at what you've written—notice the pages you've filled. Those are just some of the successes you've had in your life. Now, keeping your many impressive accomplishments in mind, take a fresh look at the things that are causing you stress today.

With your Brag Book as context, why allow worry from relatively small stressors to overtake you? Just like the 50 Stack, keep the Brag Book nearby and review it every so often. You could even browse through it before an important meeting or call.

The Future Letter

When you're going through a particularly tough or stressful time, the Future Letter is an effective tool. Gather a piece of paper and a pencil or pen. Then take a few minutes of quiet introspection before starting to write. Imagine traveling forward in time. It could be five, 10, or 30 years, whatever you think is appropriate.

Picture a future you: someone who's succeeded as much or more than you could ever imagine. Spend some time visualizing the details of this future you; let the images and sensations sink in.

When you're ready, hold onto your visualization, and write a letter from that successful future you to the current version of you.

Take a positive tone, with the goal that your future self inspires the you of today, and helps put whatever you're going through into perspective.

Here's a start to a possible future letter that can help you get going, but definitely adapt it and make it your own:

> *I know things are difficult right now but you've got what it takes. What you're going through won't last much longer, and what you're doing will pay off big-time for the rest of your life. You're doing a great job, even if doesn't always feel like it right now. You've got this.*

Let your imagination run free in this exercise. Write about how great life is for you in the future and how the sacrifice now will pay big dividends. You'll be surprised how well you can tap into the wisdom of a future you by doing this, and you can do it as often as it strikes you.

Subpersonalities

Before starting my own companies, I was a successful software executive in the United States and Europe. Back in 2003, I was hired to be a regional sales and marketing director for South East Asia, based in Singapore. Based on my accomplishments in the west, I arrived in Asia as a cocky, know-it-all 33-year-old.

Right off the bat, I told the team I inherited that I didn't care what they'd been doing before I arrived. We were going to implement the sales and marketing systems I'd used the past few years. They told me they thought that was a mistake. I plowed ahead anyway.

To make a long story short, with my lack of local knowledge, my choice not to listen to anyone, and my general arrogance, within three months, the whole team had quit. I remember the day the last person quit. I took the elevator down from the office and sat on a bench outside. I lit a cigarette and thought, *what a mess I've got myself into.* There was no one to blame but myself. I decided, *I'm going to take the rest of this cigarette to feel sorry for myself and then I'm going to suck it up and fix it.*

I made a plan to get back on track. First I would be humble. I'd own that I'd been the problem. Second, I would adapt. My processes needed to be tailored to the local cultures and customs. I would listen and get advice. I would consider what others were doing that worked.

Third, I would dedicate myself to doing whatever it took to fix things. I would handle sales myself as I filled the empty positions. I'd work late and get up early. I knew all of this would be extremely difficult. But I told myself one day I'd look back and be glad I turned a screw-up into a victory.

Then—and this is where the concept of subpersonalities comes in—I envisioned myself dressed up like Superman, complete with big muscles, and on top of my Superman outfit, I saw a suit of armor covering me up. I created an image of myself surrounded with strength and protection. Over the next few months, every time I felt the pressure getting to me, or felt beat up and defeated, I'd go back to that Superman image.

Having my Superman subpersonality to tap into made a difference—big time. I would get a shot of adrenaline, my mood would perk up, and I would be ready to go on to the next thing, almost immediately. That's the power of a subpersonality.

The idea of subpersonalities comes from a therapeutic approach called psychosynthesis. In psychosynthesis the emphasis is on integrating the various versions of ourselves into a whole, but it's also possible to conceptualize a part of ourselves having distinct traits. By creating my Superman subpersonality with certain powerful, resilient characteristics, I could call on it when I needed, and I was able to be more resilient in real life situations.

Think about how you can use subpersonalities to your benefit. Have you just been promoted to the board, yet the board meetings stress you out and you feel like a fraud? Create a subpersonality that's calm, cool, and great at strategy. Is there someone who intimidates or irritates you? Create a subpersonality that holds their own or isn't bothered. Don't like to make sales calls or talk to customers? Create a subpersonality that likes making the calls and talking to customers, and is extremely gifted at it.

- Give each subpersonality a name. It might be as simple as Board Member Ann or Confident Jake.
- Visualize this subpersonality. What are their traits? How do they act? How will they handle certain situations?
- Call them into service. When you need them, say their name in your head, and feel the power they bring.

Subpersonalities are a highly effective rewiring tool, and easy to deploy.

If you're a leader who wants to keep moving forward, you will run into imposter syndrome, self-doubt, and a critical inner voice. Using these Growth Leadership tools will allow you to quickly move past those, and get back to your confident authentic self.

CHAPTER 17:

Empathy

Studies [20] [21] [22] [23] show that empathy—the ability to understand and share the feelings of another—is one of, if not the top leadership skill. Genuinely caring about your team, vendors, and customers matters. People are significantly more engaged when they know that you care about them.

Most leaders I know want to show empathy; they just don't think it will be received well, don't want to seem "soft", or fear being taken advantage of. However, when you hold empathy back, what results is a lack of trust, a toxic culture, and poor performance. In other words, without empathy, you get the opposite of what you want.

20   The power of empathy in times of crisis and beyond (report). Catalyst. (2022). https://www.catalyst.org/reports/empathy-work-strategy-crisis

21   Radzvilavicius, A. L., Stewart, A. J., & Plotkin, J. B. (2019, April 9). Evolution of empathetic moral evaluation. eLife. https://elifesciences.org/articles/44269

22   skinner, c., & Spurgeon, P. (2016). Valuing empathy and emotional intelligence in health leadership: a study of empathy, leadership behaviour and outcome effectiveness. Sage Journals. Retrieved December 22, 2022, from https://journals.sagepub.com/doi/abs/10.1258/0951484053051924

23   Gentry, W., Weber, T., & Sadri, G. Empathy in the workplace tool for effective leadership. https://cclinnovation.org/wp-content/uploads/2020/03/empathyin-theworkplace.pdf

When somebody on your team isn't performing, being empathetic doesn't mean you overlook it or let it go. This is a case where a leader needs to be assertive and address the poor performance, while also being compassionate and honest. Come from a mindset of curiosity and focus on making the situation right, not on blaming.

Can you guess who brings more empathy to the table—a leader in their authentic self or a leader in their ego? The person in their authentic self, of course. And by handling people and situations with empathy, you'll earn trust, respect, and loyalty.

Exploration

The next time there's an issue you need to address with a team member, pause to consider an empathetic response. Keep in mind the person involved most likely had the best intentions, and was doing the best they could given their knowledge and circumstances at the time.

Instead of making it personal (i.e. emphasizing that they did something wrong), focus on finding where the problem came from and working with them to figure out a better way forward for the future.

CHAPTER 18:

Being of Service

Imagine that I told you there's a secret weapon that you can start implementing today that will:

- Give your company or team a competitive advantage
- Help you attract and retain the best employees
- Create an AMAZING culture
- Foster massive customer loyalty

And as a bonus, this secret is not only FREE, but when you use it, you'll also feel great about yourself and your life.

What I'm talking about actually exists. It's a concept that I call "being of service." The people, teams, and companies that are most focused on winning, succeeding, and making money, usually do win for a short time—but fail to do so over the long term. On the other hand, the people, teams, and companies that genuinely care about their product or service, the ones that have a purpose, care about their customers and each other—are the ones that thrive long-term.

After all, who would you be loyal to? The boss who wants to make themselves look good, and make their team #1 no matter what— or the boss who cares about customers and looks out for you as a person? It's a paradox. When you only focus on winning, you probably won't win. To be successful, you shouldn't only focus on success, you have to care. Let me give you a few real-life examples.

I was living in Copenhagen, Denmark, working at the European branch of a North American software company when two planes were flown into the World Trade Center on September 11th, 2001. Like much of the world, I was glued to the TV, watching the events unfold on CNN with horror and a sick feeling in my stomach. I turned to my Danish friend and said, "This is a day we're going to remember for the rest of our lives."

The following week was surreal and immeasurably hard. However, like all tragedies, it was also met with incredible humanity. Two days after 9/11, I was on the phone to one of my colleagues. He was stuck at our Vancouver headquarters with the rest of the sales team. At the time of the attacks, they'd been there for a multi-day sales meeting, but now all air travel was frozen.

I asked him what was going on there. He said, "We're all pretty shocked, though Ken has been on the phone non-stop." Ken was a senior salesperson who I'd always looked up to, both as a business-person and as a human being. He was the guy who always crushed his numbers yet was universally liked, and he was incredibly generous with his time to everyone.

I replied, "Really, why? Who's he talking to?" At a time like this, no one was going to be thinking about the multi-million dollar accounting software we sold.

"He's reaching out to all his customers and prospects and checking in. But he isn't selling. He's asking if they're OK, if anyone they know got caught in the attacks, and letting them know that he's thinking about them and their families."

Frankly, 31-year-old Michael didn't understand this. "What are they saying?" I asked, confused.

"They're so appreciative. Ken's been talking to some of them for an hour—not business, just person to person." That's the type of person Ken was. He cared. He was being of service. It wasn't about money; it wasn't about making a sale. It was about genuinely connecting with people. It took me quite a few years to understand the compassion Ken was demonstrating, and why everyone liked and respected him so much.

Here's another example. John Wooden, the former UCLA college basketball coach who won 10 national championships and a record 88 consecutive games, never talked about winning. He talked about playing hard and giving your all. He taught the team the proper skills, and they won more than anyone else—without focusing on winning.

When the team played hard in a game, yet they lost, he would be happy and proud of them. When the team was lazy and undisciplined, but they won, he would get angry and point out what needed to change. That's because actions like playing hard, being disciplined, and putting the team first are things you can control. By focusing on what can be controlled, the team went on to win much more than lose.

In business, this is just as true, if not more true than it is in sports.

If you've travelled by plane a lot in the United States, you probably have been on a flight with Southwest Airlines. While it's a low-cost airline, you may have noticed that everyone working there is just simply *nice*. The leader who took Southwest from a tiny company to a major player is Herb Kelleher. Herb always preached that "if you take care of your employees, they'll take care of the customer."

He was a great listener; he was humble, had a great sense of humor, and he was always keen to learn, even if it was from a rookie flight attendant. When Southwest went through tough times, he took personal pay cuts and sold planes instead of laying people off.

On Bosses Day a few years ago, the 16,000 employees of Southwest chipped in to purchase a full-page ad in *USA Today* to thank Herb for, among other things, "helping load bags on Thanksgiving, singing at the holiday party and singing only once a year, letting them wear shorts and sneakers to work, being a friend, not just a boss, and remembering every one of their names."[24]

I've flown a lot in my life, and Southwest is the ONLY discount airline I'll fly—and it's because of how kind the people who work there are. When I get onto a Southwest flight, I'm usually one of the first ones on board—at 6 feet 8 inches tall, I pay extra to get in first for a seat with good legroom—and I like to ask the flight attendants how they like working there. Every single one likes, if not loves it, and the ones who've been there longer speak highly of Herb. Many of them recall times when they chatted personally with him on a flight or at an event.

(Recent update: In late December 2022, Southwest Airlines, 21 years after Herb stepped down as CEO, had to cancel thousands of flights and stranding many people over the holiday period, due to IT breakdowns. It will be interesting to see how the current management responds to this latest challenge.)

In today's world, it's hard if not impossible to differentiate most products or services. Yet when you can earn the loyalty and devotion of your employees, and ensure excellent customer satisfaction, you'll become much more successful. You do this by being of service to these people—employees, customers, and—ultimately—everyone.

---

24   Freiberg, K & J. (2019). *20 Reasons Why Herb Kelleher Was One Of The Most Beloved Leaders Of Our Time.* https://www.forbes.com/sites/kevinandjackiefreiberg/2019/01/04/20-reasons-why-herb-kelleher-was-one-of-the-most-beloved-leaders-of-our-time/

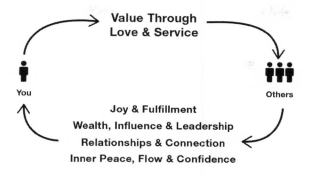

Figure 14: The Law of Value

Care about your team and they'll care about you, the company, and the customers. Treat them like a paid employee, and they'll do their job, get their paycheck…and that's about it.

I call this the Law of Value (Figure 14). When we give value through love and service, we appreciate our team for giving their all to the company and our customers because ultimately, we're there to serve them. By giving freely from this pure energy, you'll find that things come back to you automatically—more joy, fulfillment, wealth, and influence.

This applies to relationships and connections too; you become influential when people see this authentic, non-ego-based intention within you. And if you believe in a higher power—the universe, Nature, God, Allah, Buddha or something else bigger than ourselves—you might say that service is a manifestation of that. If I want to be happy, one of the quickest, best ways to do that is to make somebody else happy.

Here's a great quote about service from the book *Letting Go* by David Hawkins: *"As our consciousness grows, we see that service, which is living oriented toward others, automatically results in the fulfillment of our own needs. (This does not mean sacrifice. Service is not sacrifice.)"*

Being of service should feel easy and flow naturally. When you're in the zone, it doesn't feel like hard work. Even if you're working hard, it's on behalf of other people, and that makes it much more palatable. Work becomes not just what you do, but how you do it and the energy behind it. Then you wind up attracting people who share the same beliefs—not just people in it for a paycheck.

That said, being of service doesn't mean bending over backwards to give everybody what they want. That's people pleasing. You need super-clear boundaries—after all, how can you give great service to everyone, everywhere? You can't. And when it comes to your team, being of service can equally be about challenging them, bringing out their best, and even confronting them when they veer off course.

Exploration

Think of your customers. What value do you provide to them? How are you being of service to them? Are there areas where you are sacrificing how you serve them to make more profit? Is that good for the long term?

Think of your employees. Do you understand the lives of your employees, and make decisions that balance the company's interests with their interests? Are your employees being of service to your customers?

Think of any other stakeholders (vendors, partners, investors, volunteers, etc.) Are you in service to them?

CHAPTER 19:

The Owner versus Victim Choice

In any situation, you have a simple choice. You can take ownership of the situation or you can fall into victimhood. When you take ownership, you're there to solve whatever the problem is—no blame, no complaints, you just fix it. When you play the victim, you focus on proving that the problem isn't your fault and passing it off to someone else. Being the victim is an ego-based reaction. The ego doesn't ever want to take responsibility or admit fault.

Standing in your full ownership is what earns the respect of other people—your staff, peers, and managers, if you have any. It sets the tone for your team. Many leaders tell me they want to create a great culture, yet they're not taking 100% ownership. They're still making excuses and trying to put responsibility on other people's shoulders when it actually belongs on their own.

I know an executive coach who was working with the CEO of a medium-sized business. That CEO wasn't getting along with his top-producing salesperson, even though he'd worked with her for years. They argued frequently, often in front of other employees. The coach tried working with each of them individually, but couldn't get them on the same page—and the relationship kept getting worse and worse. One day the CEO came in and told the coach, "That's it. I'm going to fire her. She's creating a toxic workplace and I'm tired of it."

At the time, the salesperson in question was responsible for 60% of new product sales. Clearly, if the CEO followed through on firing her, it would set his company back significantly.

Knowing this, the coach made a suggestion, "You know what, this is an important decision. There's one more thing I think is worth trying...I think you should apologize to her."

You can guess the CEO's reaction, "Why should I apologize to her? She's the one who's the problem. I'm the boss, she should respect me. This is my company."

"Well," said the coach, holding up the roster of employees, "which half of these employees are you going to lay off? Because that's what you're going to have to do when you fire her." With a deep sigh the CEO said, "OK, so what does me apologizing to her look like?"

That next day the CEO asked the salesperson to lunch. She agreed, guessing it was her last day. After the awkward drive to the restaurant, and ordering their meals, the CEO took a deep breath and dove in.

"You know what, I want to admit something. You're bringing in sales and you're good at your job. My job is to support you, and instead of doing that, I've been acting like a jerk. Now I'm going to apologize. I've been acting childish and stupid, and I'm sorry. I want to know how I can be a better boss, and how I can support you better going forward."

The CEO said the next 10 seconds were the longest of his life as she just stared at him. Then, she started crying. She said, "Thank you. Thank you so much. I've been acting like a child too. I like working here, and we had a bunch of good years together before this. I would love to get back on the same page!"

From there, they came together. They had a phenomenal lunch, where she shared all the great ideas she'd never brought up before because he wouldn't listen. Fast forward a few years, she's now VP of Sales, and the company is scaling up even faster than before.

This story is a prime example of what awareness, responding from the authentic self, and taking ownership look like. The CEO knew he couldn't control his salesperson—but he could control how he showed up. He put aside his ego in order to help propel the company forward. It was a risk, since he didn't know how she would respond, but by swallowing his pride and owning his responsibility, so did she. When you take full, unrestrained ownership, other people almost always step up to own their part too.

To see if someone's showing up as an owner or a victim, look at the language they're using. "I'll be happy when..." is a common victim's refrain. *I'll be happy when I make six figures. I'll be happy when I lose weight. I'll be happy when I get married. I'll be happy when I have kids. I'll be happy when I get divorced.* The goal posts are always moving. People in victim mode are always waiting for external circumstances to change. But the fact is, happiness is created. Happiness is a choice. Happiness is available right here, right now, regardless of circumstance.

Someone deep in victimhood might also say, "Oh, I was going to do that, but I didn't have time." Well, if three days go by, and that task didn't take 72 hours, then it would be more accurate to say that they chose to make other things a priority. "I didn't have time" is usually a statement of victimhood. Poor time management, missing deadlines, and excuses are all victimhood behaviors.

Here's an example of how your choices can shape people's opinions of you. Once I was leading a breakout session at a conference, and a colleague came in a few minutes before start time. The main session wrapped up late, and people were milling around outside, so I started the breakout session a few minutes late to accommodate people finding their seats.

After the breakout, I asked what my colleague thought. He said, "Mike, I liked the content, but I feel you let me down a little bit." I was somewhat surprised. "Why is that, Scott?"

He said, "It was disappointing that you started late."

"Yes, there were a lot of people still walking around outside and I wanted to give them a chance to get in and get settled," I explained.

"I understand that," he said. "But I made it on time. So, it's my time that you wasted, and it's my time you didn't respect, even though I was the one that made the effort." After reflecting on this, the lesson came through loud and clear. I apologized to Scott and thanked him, because he was absolutely right.

When a few people make it on time to your meeting but you wait for a few others to arrive before you start, you're sending the message that being on time isn't important. If you want a culture of high-performance, trust, and respect, you have to become extremely aware of everything you do as a leader. It isn't always easy or comfortable to show up in ownership mode, and it can be even more uncomfortable to call out other people who are playing the victim, but it's necessary.

Scientifically, studies show that people who take ownership not only have more physical and mental energy[25]—they're more cre-

---

25   Optimism: Definition and research. Leadership IQ. https://www.leadership-iq.com/blogs/leadershipiq/optimism

ative and productive[26]. That's the fuel that leads to more success and stronger leadership. Leaders don't complain or play victim, they focus on actions, solutions, and figuring things out. They're positive, strategic, and proactive. And importantly, they're accountable. If they don't know how to do something, they find out or figure it out.

In each of the roles you play in your life, you're almost certainly playing victim somewhere in a relationship or situation. The ego loves this because it loves negativity. It loves entitlement. It loves to get defensive and place blame, saying things like, *I can't. I don't know. I should, but...*

So, how do you switch from victim to owner? You can do it in a split second. And like everything else, it starts with awareness. Once you have that, choosing a stronger response follows. This applies to any situation, event, conversation, or relationship. The key is to base your response on what you can control, and disregard any factors beyond that.

In recent years, there's been an increased amount of chaos around the world—public health crises, climate, economic and political challenges, and more. A lot of people started spinning out of control. However, leaders who thrived asked questions like, "How do we need to change and adapt?" "What difficult decisions do I need to make right now?" "What new opportunities are available that we can target?"

Train yourself to look out for language or behaviors that indicate someone falling into victimhood. Notice when it comes up in others, and especially when it comes up for you—even in your self-talk. When you catch yourself, don't get down, judge yourself,

---

26   Frost, S. (2021). Optimism at work: Developing and validating scales to measure workplace optimism. https://aura.antioch.edu/cgi/viewcontent. cgi?article=1713&context=etds

or stay in any negativity. Have some compassion. Then choose a stronger response…and move on.

Exploration

What do you complain about? What do you wish was different?

Keeping those answers in mind, where and how are you playing the victim?

How can you shift into ownership? What does that look like?

CHAPTER 20:

The Psychology of Procrastination

How often do you have a potentially life-changing idea? You get a vision to start a new company, write a book, or finally start that YouTube channel you've been talking about for years. However, you never get past the talking or the planning stage. Even though you think about this idea all the time, it never gets off the ground.

This applies to both big ideas and more ordinary things like eating less meat or working out. Or, it could be something you resist, like having a difficult conversation with your new employee who's been late three times this week. No matter what it is, it takes up mental energy, gnawing at you—a reminder that you're not moving forward despite knowing better.

Procrastination is pervasive...and procrastination sucks.

Pause for a minute and think of one place in your life where you're procrastinating. Now put that in your back pocket. We'll come back to it in a few minutes. You're about to learn exactly where most procrastination comes from and how you can overcome it each and every time.

When children are in the developmental stage between 3-6 years old, there's one main thing that they want in life. It's the love and adoration of their caregivers. No secret there, right? What kids want is love and acceptance.

Let's imagine I'm four years old, at a picnic, and I'm in a race with 100 other kids. My dad, who loves me and wants to make sure I grow up to be a tough man, is on the sideline watching. The race starts and I run as fast as I can, and I come in…third. Third out of 100. Pretty good, right?

Can you guess what my father said to me? "Michael, what's wrong with you? We don't lose! You're not putting your heart into it. Pump your arms faster!"

"OK Dad, I got it. Just wait until next time!"

A few hours later, I'm in another race with 100 other kids. The race starts, and I put my whole heart into it. I pump my arms as hard as I can and I come in…second.

What does my dad say this time – is he happy? Of course not. He wants to teach me to win and not settle for anything less.

"Second place? First loser! You have to try harder to win. I'm so disappointed in you."

Now, keep in mind that at the age of four, what I care about most is my dad's love and acceptance. What internal connection do I make from my experience in those races that day? *Winning equals acceptance. When I win, and come in first, I'll be loved.*

Now imagine it's a year later, and I just took a test at school and got every question right. I run in the house, excited to show my mom. "Wow, you got 100% right! I'm so proud of you. I love you so much!"

What's the internal connection you imagine I made this time? *Perfection equals love. When everything is just right then I'm worthy and lovable.* When a child gets this type of conditioning in their developmental years, the next time they have a choice between challenging themselves and taking a hard test, or playing it safe and taking an easy test, what would you imagine they'd do? *They take the easy test; there's a higher chance of getting 100%.*

The next time they have the choice between taking an easy test or no test at all, what do you think they'd do? *They almost certainly choose to avoid the test because then there's no chance of not getting 100%. They avoid the risk of being less than worthy, less than lovable.*

If this sounds familiar, you're not alone. This type of parenting is called *conditional parenting* and it's very common. Although your parents wanted the best for you, now we know this can lead to unhelpful thoughts and behavior patterns. This is where procrastination comes from.

Now, let's go back to what you're procrastinating about—the thing you put in your back pocket at the beginning of this chapter. Whatever it is, let's examine it and consider the fact that there must be a reason you're putting it off.

How is you procrastinating on that thing your version of choosing to take no test? How are you playing it safe by not getting that done? This might be a blind spot—it is for many people—so no beating yourself up if you can't answer right away. Just know that there's a way in which procrastinating has served you and your old wiring.

What you've just learned about procrastination applies to most cases, especially at work. But there are also other types of procrastination, for example, not sticking to a diet, not listening to doctor's orders, and other personal care habits that are more likely to be driven by self-limiting beliefs.

Many competitive people find that the older they get, and the more successful they are, the less they want to take risks. Psychologically, we don't want to put ourselves in a position where we can fail and knock down the tower of success that our identity loves so much.

How does this apply to your own life, and leadership? Maybe you avoid risks—projects that aren't guaranteed to work. Or perhaps you're a perfectionist, putting off crucial decisions because you don't have all the information needed to decide. Or, you don't release a new product until it's totally bug free, which delays it for months or years. Do you refuse to delegate something because your ego gets a sense of importance and worth every time you do it? Remember, procrastination is another way the ego is fighting, in its own way, to protect you through avoiding change and exposure.

Here's a very fast hack for getting through procrastination, taking on risky projects, and keeping you and your team resilient. It's to frame things as *experiments*. This helps because it takes all the pressure off of being perfect or "right." If you have to have a conversation with someone that you're avoiding—maybe it's a cold call, an angry client, or an investor—figure out your approach to the call, then frame the whole process as an experiment. You're going to see what part of it works and what part of it doesn't.

There's so much less stress in doing it this way, and you also adopt more of a learning and growth mindset around it all. Besides, what's the only way to fail in an experiment? To not try it at all.

Exploration

Pick an area in your life where you're procrastinating.

Why are you doing that? What's the payoff to your ego?

How can you take ownership of the situation and move forward? What's a small experiment you can try?

CHAPTER 21:

Balancing Your Leadership

My experience has shown time and again that leaders are either naturally driven or naturally supportive[27]. The individual leader's growth comes through learning how to balance their innate gifts while developing their less dominant side.

Driven people are the type to come up with a big vision and take big risks. They tend to be more competitive, achievement and goal-oriented, disciplined, and confident. People who are naturally wired to be more supportive, on the other hand, love being on a team and doing their part for that team. They tend to be extremely empathetic and compassionate, nurturing, and have strong intuition.

Driven people often find themselves in leadership positions because they step forward more often, and sometimes put themselves before the team. Supportive people make just as good leaders, however, it may not be as natural to them to go for that promotion or start a company.

Any high-performing team has a mix of both driven and supportive people, and high-performing leaders are usually able to be strong on both sides, even if one is dominant.

---

[27] I'm using the terms "Driven" and "Supportive" here, however, these aspects are normally referred to as "Masculine" and "Feminine" in psychology. I've changed them here to be more accessible and avoid any confusion.

Each personality type has a healthy and an unhealthy aspect to it. On the healthy side, the supportive person tends to be the glue holding things together, while the driven person pushes things forward. You can see some more typical traits for each of these types in Figure 15.

	SUPPORTIVE	DRIVEN
UNHEALTHY	• People Pleaser, Lack Boundaries • Victim, Burnout • Martyr, Self-sacrificing • Insecure - Outside Validation • Needy	• Bully, Critical • Narcissistic • Cold & Distant • Insecure - Distance, Closed, Aggressive
HEALTHY	• Nurturing, Vulnerable • Caring, Compassionate • Clear Boundaries • Confident - Authentic, Intuitive	• Goal Achieving • Focused, Disciplined • Strong, Creates Safety • Confident - Empowering, Authentic

Figure 15: Supportive and Driven Leadership Aspects

When leaders come under pressure and fall into ego-driven behavior, that's when the unhealthy traits will start to appear. With driven people, that looks like bullying, criticism, narcissism, aggression, insecurity, and becoming cold and distant. For the supportive types, this shows up through people-pleasing, poor boundaries, burnout, martyrdom, self-sacrificing, and needing validation.

Looking at yourself through the "driven versus supportive" lens, what are your observations? When you get tired, the pressure is on, and you're dealing with too much, what behaviors creep in?

If you are typically driven and competitive, those are great traits, however you don't want to overuse them. You probably tend to over-focus on goals and winning, pushing forward with a "win at all costs" mentality, and that causes issues in your work (and personal) life. To balance your leadership, you need to slow down, and work on your relationships by building deeper connections.

If you identify as the supportive type, you show your care to others and take a lot of pride in your work. To develop as a balanced leader, it will be important to learn to take care of yourself first, otherwise, you'll tend towards people-pleasing and shaky boundaries. Your growth will come from asserting yourself in the right way in the right situations, holding people accountable, getting better with conflict, and embodying more executive presence.

These are the choices in front of you as you rewire and reprogram yourself as a leader.

As a naturally driven person, I have amazing discipline and focus, but when I get stressed, and my ego goes unchecked, I can become critical of myself and other people. I become cold, distant, and narcissistic, but I know that about myself, so my growth as a leader has come from changing my responses. I also work continuously to strengthen my ability to be caring and compassionate; I make time to slow down, focus on being authentic, intuitive, and vulnerable.

Recently, I went through a five-month healing journey with prostate cancer—for the second time. At first, when I heard about the therapy I'd be having, I thought to myself, *I'm strong. I will be able to work as normal through most of the treatment.* As the treatment date got closer, I even thought I'd work right up to the first day of treatment and then, the day after, I could start working again. My wiring as a driven personality was revealing itself.

As I experienced the intense hormone and radiation therapy, I realized that I needed to take every single to-do and responsibility off my plate (except one project that I could do whenever I had the energy), and let go of any timetable for when I would be back working again.

Everything I'd built up over the last few years—all the clients, the marketing and sales, the masterminds, trainings and coaching—had to be put on hold without a return date, and would lose momentum. It took me a few weeks to get my head around it, but once I did and had a totally clean calendar and to-do list—I felt so free. Once I let go of trying to drive things, and developed the traits from my non-dominant side, my inner life (and therefore my outer life) became so much easier.

Great leaders are able to show up with healthy behaviors from both the driven and supportive sides of themselves. Then, those leaders apply this understanding to their teams. Pause for a moment and consider the key people on your team—are they wired to be driven or supportive? If you have a clear answer, now you know how to coach them to be their best. Help them see when they drift into the unhealthy behaviors. You can even sit down and teach them what you just learned, share this book with them, and empower them to develop a plan so they can work on the healthy side of their non-dominant aspect. That's how you as a leader can nurture leadership in the people around you.

A driven, high achiever who also knows how to demonstrate vulnerability and empathy is virtually unstoppable. And a highly intuitive supportive person who also taps into their focus, discipline, and confidence will likewise become extremely powerful.

Exploration

What's your natural style—driven or supportive?

What triggers send you into an unhealthy state? Do certain people or situations bring out your worst?

What does it look and feel like when you start to enter either of the unhealthy states? Does your voice change? Do you feel tightness in your chest? Do you get lightheaded? What signs can you can identify in your body?

Look at the traits of your non-dominant style. How can you develop more of those?

CHAPTER 22:

The Two Pyramids of Leadership

As a leader, you will run into many different dichotomies—two seemingly opposite ideas that are both true—and it's up to you to discern which one is relevant at any given moment. In this chapter, we'll look at one of those dichotomies: how you view your role as a leader. We'll use two opposing pyramids to illustrate different approaches to leadership. Each is true and valid. I want you to have both in your toolkit so you can apply the one you need at any given time.

The Pyramid of Values

In the Pyramid of Values (Figure 16: Pyramid of Values), we see you at the top, your company and team below you, and your individual team members at the bottom. In this configuration, your number one priority is yourself. The rationale for this is that it's your responsibility to make sure you're healthy, sane and clear-headed so you can look after all the people you bear responsibility for. It's also up to you to know your values. If your company, or any team member underneath you diverges from those values, then it's your job to stand your ground, even if it means having difficult conversations or making difficult choices.

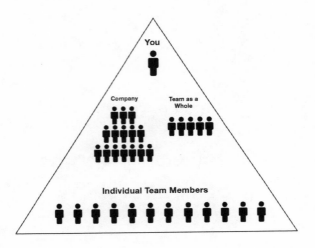

Figure 16: Pyramid of Values

On the next level down, the company and your team sit side by side, and the individual team members at the bottom of this pyramid. The team and the company are more important than any one person. It's your job to create and sustain an amazing team, and if one person's attitude, skillset, or values aren't in line with what you are leading, then they cannot be part of the team.

In addition, you need to make sure that the company stays healthy and successful, because a thriving company means you can serve more people in the long run. This can drive decisions such as making layoffs when an economic downturn happens. They are very difficult moves to make, but as a leader you need to make sure the company survives so that it can be a force for good in the future.

Your loyalty is always to yourself first. Make sure you don't compromise your values or health, even for the team or the company. Then, you also need to make sure your team has a strong culture and the company is healthy. If there are any individuals who are not serving you, your team, or company, that needs to be addressed.

In the previous chapter, you learned about the supportive and driven personality types. Often I've found that supportive type leaders grow when they learn and apply this mindset to their leadership.

Here's a quick story to illustrate this. My software company hired the services of a human resources firm that handled everything from payroll to health insurance—the latter becomes a real headache when your business grows, especially in the United States. You have to deal with different rates and regulations across various states and at the local, state, and federal levels.

All our employees had to sign standard documents with this firm, but one person kicked up a fuss. There was one sentence in a sea of legalese that he had a problem with. We took his concern to the HR firm. They let us know that hundreds of thousands of employees had signed that document, and that to their knowledge no one had ever had an issue with that single sentence. They couldn't strike the sentence from our employee's contract.

After weeks of this issue taking up a lot of my time as CEO, I told my executive coach, Michelle, that I wanted to show the employee that I cared about them. To do that, I was going to cancel the contract with the HR firm—even though we'd spent the better part of a year selecting them.

She disagreed. At first I didn't understand. "Why? I want to make sure all my employees know I care about them and will go out of my way for them."

"I understand." she said. "Though let me ask you this. Do you treat them well?"

"Yes," I replied. I paid well and provided great benefits, coaching, growth opportunities, and a nurturing, caring culture. In fact, the plan was for this HR firm to add new benefits in different areas, part of the reason my company was named one of the "Top 5 Best Places to Work" for a few years.

My coach continued, "Since you've already created such a positive culture, you can be comfortable with what you're offering—as long as it's aligned with what you think is right. In this case, someone's being a squeaky wheel. Don't set a precedent that squeaky wheels get the grease. As the leader, you see the big picture, and it's okay to expect people to be team players. It's your job to do what's right for everyone."

Thanks to her coaching, I understood the importance of getting clear about my values as a leader, what my company was about, and what kind of people made good teammates. After I decided not to accommodate him, and serve the team as a whole instead, that employee chose to take a job elsewhere.

At our next quarterly meeting two weeks later, I went over the situation—our thought process, what we did to accommodate him while keeping our benefits at a high level—but that ultimately it wasn't right for him. I took time to ask if anyone had any questions or comments, which no one did, and afterwards, in some private conversations, I discovered that no one was particularly bothered that he'd left. While he was talented, he could be difficult to work with.

Remember, I'd been ready to cancel the entire HR contract and take us back to the drawing board because of this single person's input. From my vantage point at the top of the Pyramid of Values, I was able to make a decision that put the team as a whole ahead of an individual. When you're in a situation like that, having a coach—someone who listens compassionately to you without judgment and helps you come up with your own path forward—can be a game-changer.

Exploration

Where are your values not aligned with someone you're working with?

Are you making sure you're healthy on the mental, emotional, and physical levels, so you can be the best for your team and company?

The Pyramid of Service

Let's now look at the **Pyramid of Service** (Figure 17).

In this case, we take the typical organizational chart and invert it. In this upside-down pyramid, your place as the leader is at the bottom—the exact opposite of the Pyramid of Values. Why?

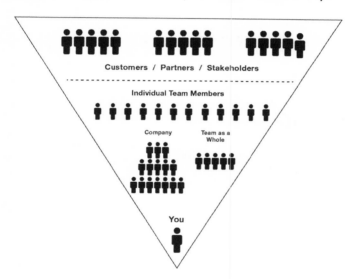

Figure 17: Pyramid of Service

This configuration, made popular in the concept of Servant Leadership by Robert Greenleaf, positions you as the person who empowers everyone else in the pyramid, including the customer at the top. The sales reps, customer service, and support people who are

175

on the frontline are also near the top, close to the customers, partners and other stakeholders. You are in service to, or supporting, everyone else above you.

Highly driven leaders often find more growth and success by learning and applying this model to their leadership.

If this is your first time considering your company and your leadership in this formation, you might find it refreshing. You're no longer at the top; you're there to make sure everybody has everything that they need to serve their stakeholders. Your role is to enable others to perform, to ensure they have the right training and the right mindset; and that the right culture is in place so individuals can do their best. When your team does a great job, you're doing a great job, and your company thrives. You serve your team, and your team and your company are there to serve each person in your company, who are there to serve the customers.

Exploration

Think about who you serve and how you serve them—members of your team, customers, and even your family.

How can you shift your mindset to show up in greater service to them?

CHAPTER 23:

YOU are the Hero

There's a man many people have never heard of but whose work touches our lives more than most—Joseph Campbell. While he calls himself a "mythologist," Campbell was first a psychologist who studied under Carl Jung, who in turn was a student of Sigmund Freud. Then, following his interest in mythology, Campbell started studying the stories of different religions, which led to an amazing revelation: every religion tells the same story.

In his groundbreaking book, *A Hero of a Thousand Faces,* he dives into what he calls the Hero's Journey (Figure 18: The Hero's Journey), which breaks down the path any ordinary human takes to achieve the big goal they seek to achieve in life. Along the way, there are obstacles and challenges, as well as help in the form of mentors, and of course, the person grows enormously—transforming into a hero by the time they return from the quest.

The Hero's Journey is the backbone of almost every television show, movie, and book out there. In fact, when George Lucas was writing *Star Wars*, he read Campbell's book, stopped work on the script, hired Campbell as a writing consultant, and re-wrote the story to follow the Hero's Journey.

The reason the Hero's Journey is so attractive to viewers and readers is that it mirrors our own lives, specifically, how we view ourselves in our own journeys. When we understand what we need to go through as a human to grow and evolve, it reminds us to keep everything in perspective, adding to our confidence, resilience, and power.

Let's break down the Hero's Journey by going through the plot of *Star Wars: A New Hope* (the very first movie released in 1977). Even if you didn't see it or don't remember it well, you can follow the arc.

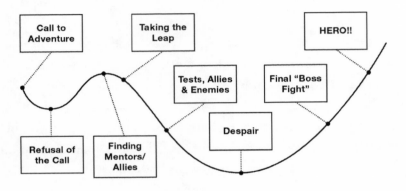

Figure 18: The Hero's Journey

The story always starts out with a reluctant hero, an everyday, ordinary type of person we can all relate to, who is "called to adventure." In *Star Wars,* Luke Skywalker was just a farm boy out on his aunt and uncle's farm. Remember how he wanted to join the rebel fleet?

The call to adventure is refused at first—Luke's aunt and uncle told him that they needed him on the farm and he couldn't go. Despite refusing the call, the hero is then thrown into the adventure. In the case of Luke, his aunt and uncle are murdered and he was thrust into the fight. Like all heroes do, Luke finds mentors and allies, including Obi Wan Kenobi, R2D2, C3P0, Han Solo, Chewbacca, and Princess Leia.

The hero also faces many tests. In *Star Wars* there are many, from the cantina to infiltrating the Death Star and rescuing the Princess. Throughout the journey, the hero has a flaw; a weak point they never address. The story reaches a climax, a point of despair when it looks like the hero is about to die. However, the hero digs deep inside, musters all of their strength, and overcomes this flaw.

Luke's flaw was not trusting his instincts. But towards the end of the journey, when he was about to blow up the Death Star with Darth Vader on his tail, instead of using the computer targeting system, he switches to manual mode, trusts himself, and succeeds at making the miracle shot—overcoming his flaw and becoming a true hero.

The Hero's Journey is the story of our lives. We've all had things not work out. We've all taken leaps and we've all failed. In my case, I went through a divorce and substance abuse. I had an alcoholic father. These things made me strong, and made me who I am. Part of the reason I'm successful is that I've learned from the challenges I encountered on my journey and used the lessons to my advantage.

Your walk through the Hero's Journey will happen many times in your life in different ways. If you get promoted, that may be you as a reluctant hero getting the initial call to adventure. But the same could be said of starting a business or meeting a future spouse. These are all hero's journeys.

The most important moment in the journey is the "Point of Despair." When things are at their worst, when everything's stacked against you, and when you just want to give up—what do you do? The hero—that's you—digs down deep and to prove what they're made of. Anyone can lead when everything's going well. It's during the difficult times—the crises, the recessions, the layoffs, the lawsuits—that your character and reputation are built. How you show up when the chips are down is what people remember.

Everyone has their demons. The ironic thing is that what you hate most about your past has likely shaped your character *in a good way*—even more than your other experiences. If you had a storybook upbringing, one with no problems or difficulties, where you got everything you wanted with the perfect mom and dad, you wouldn't be who you are now.

Are you driven? Do you have compassion and empathy? Are you resilient? Those things come from living through hardships. Whether it's a dysfunctional family, overcoming your own substance abuse or a prior business failure, these experiences have strengthened you and taught you lessons you couldn't have learned elsewhere.

Just think…what if you had to go through all of that to be the person—the leader—you are now? To take you, your team, and your company to the next level? Would you view your life differently? Yes, of course you would. And you should.

A hero isn't someone who has superpowers. They're someone who does amazing things to help people. Start looking at your life through the lens of the Hero's Journey—not only accepting, but embracing everything that got you here—and choose to be the hero everyone's waiting for.

Exploration

What do you judge and regret about your life? How has that helped shape how you are now?

Keeping that in mind, how does the Hero's Journey apply to you?

What if everything you've been through in your life is preparing you for right now?

The Growth Leadership Path

Phase 3: Leading Others

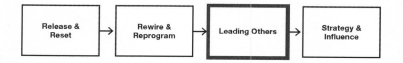

Since your leadership is a reflection of the relationship with yourself, until this point we've focused on redefining that relationship. You've cleared out false beliefs and insecurities and filled that space with truth and confidence. However leadership, at the end of the day, is about leading others, and that's what we'll cover next.

When you're working to change your *own* mindset, the advantage is that you have control over yourself, whereas when you're managing and leading others, you can only influence them. Everyone has their own personality, values, and goals, and it takes a combination of science and art to get a group of people working in the same direction. What works with one person one day may not work with another person—or even the same person—on the next day.

Once you've deployed what you learn in this phase of the Growth Leadership Path, the team will take on a life of its own. You may even reach the point where they'll figure out complex problems, hold each other accountable, and take full responsibility, all without your oversight, which is your end objective.

You might have concerns about your team becoming completely independent, asking yourself *"what if they no longer need me?"* Don't worry. Everyone always knows who the leader is. If you're authentic and you lead from a place of service, the people on your team will have lifelong loyalty and respect for you, and you'll be working on what you should be—strategy and the big picture.

You will want to go more slowly as you integrate what you learn in these next chapters. If you have an existing team, you'll need to figure out how to implement the suggested changes. Don't read a chapter and the next day announce to your team that there's a new way of working, as that could backfire. A lot of change at once for any group can cause fear and resistance. Go forward mindfully.

As you proceed, your patience will pay off because once you create a high-performing team, the transformation is remarkable. People form tight bonds, trust is created, great value is produced, you exceed your targets, and everyone grows as people.

CHAPTER 24:

Unbreakable Commitments

If I asked you what a commitment is, how would you answer? Most people say it's something you will do. And when they say that, they mean something they will probably do, intend to do, or might do.

For example, how many times have you told someone you would send them some information on Tuesday, then wake up early Wednesday and send it then—thinking *well, that's close enough.* After all, it's practically still Tuesday and Wednesday hasn't even started yet.

Or, you're set to meet someone for coffee at 11:00 AM. You forgot to allow extra time to park and you roll up at 11:03. Again, you think *well, close enough. I didn't know there would be traffic.*

How about when you randomly bump into an old colleague on the street? After a greeting and some small talk, you say, "I'll give you a ring and we'll catch up for lunch one day." Yet you both know you have no intention of actually doing that.

All of these are examples of failed commitments. The actual definition of a commitment (according to the Cambridge dictionary) is *a promise or firm decision to do something.* That means it's something you're 100% going to follow through and do. Anything else is a failed commitment.

In the first two examples, try reversing the positions. If someone promises to send you something one day, and you get it the next morning, what do you think? Or if someone is a few minutes late to a business meeting, do you notice? Personally, I have a little score-card in my head for any given person. If they miss a commitment, they lose a tiny bit of trust on my scorecard. I may never bring it up, but on a certain level I'm evaluating people on their character. To me, making a commitment and not following through demonstrates a lack of integrity, and it's the same for a lot of high-level leaders. Even if they don't show it, they take notice of these things in order to evaluate people's integrity.

The good news is, when you DO deliver what you say you'll do, you get a positive on the scorecard...by simply living up to expectations.

In this chapter, we're going to get clear on making unbreakable commitments and how this will strengthen not only your leadership, but your relationship to yourself, your relationship with others, and the culture of your team. In most cases, we'll do this by making a lot fewer commitments while we get crystal clear on what those commitments are—and are not. People who've been through my courses and masterminds find that tightening up their commitments is one of the fastest, strongest wins available.

We've established that a commitment is not something that you might do, or sort-of do. What else is a commitment not? A commitment is not a goal. A goal is something you hope to do that's usually aspirational. A commitment is something you absolutely will do and you know that you can reasonably make happen.

I once had a new marketing assistant. Each time I assigned him a task, he would ask me when I wanted it done by. I would ask him by when he could commit to doing it. He would then tell me a day and I would say, "That's fine." Three times in a row we went through that process, and each time, on the day it was due, he would get all flustered and tell me, "I can't get it done by today, I need more time!" After the third time, I stopped him and we had a talk.

I gave him my commitment speech and told him that he wasn't giving me his commitment date, he was giving me his goal date. He *wanted* to get things done by that date—and was probably giving me an earlier date to try and impress me. Can you see how he was making things difficult for himself and eroding the trust I had in him? To his credit, he took that on board and changed his behavior. After that, he gave me realistic commitments and hit every one, and my trust in him grew and grew.

It can be funny to see how people make commitments without thinking them through first. Say I'm coaching a client and they want to get into shape. Here's what the conversation might look like:

Client: *I'm ready to get back into running.*

Me: *OK, so what will you commit to?*

Client: *Easy, I'll run an hour a day, every day, for the next two weeks.*

Me: *Wow. That's amazing. So when's the last time you ran, or worked out at all?*

Client: *It's been a while—probably two years.*

Me: *Hmmm… if that's the case, an hour a day may be overdoing it, don't you think?*

Client: *Yes, probably.*

Me: *Also, tell me. Over the next two weeks, do you have anything planned?*

Client: *Ah, yes. Next week I go to Frankfurt for a yearly conference.*

Me: *Interesting. Will you be busy at the conference?*

Client: *Yes, it's all-consuming. From the minute I wake up until late at night.*

Me: *So, you may not be able to work out every single day for the next two weeks, will you?*

Client: ...

This is actually a very common scenario. People want to push themselves and make aspirational proclamations when it comes to commitments. However, being unrealistic only leads to anxiety, broken promises, and lack of trust.

When you're making a commitment, think about what you'll need to do in order to fulfill it. Are you very busy? If so, have you set a realistic timeline? What will you have to take off your plate or rearrange? Is that truly in your control? Are you leaving any slack time if an emergency pops up, or if things don't go to plan? If not, start to do that so your commitment becomes real.

This is something you can—and should—teach your team as well. If you want high performance, your team needs to learn to make rock-solid commitments and then deliver on them. Otherwise, the culture of trust you want just won't develop.

Of course, this all starts with you, and applies to the little things. A CEO hired me to run a strategy session with them. They sent over a packet of their plans and goals so I could get up to speed with what they'd been doing. As we sat down to start I said, "Before we get too far into planning, I have a question about what you sent me."

"What's that?" asked the CEO.

"One of your core values is 'tight.' What does that mean?" I enquired.

"Ah," said the CEO. "That means, for example, everyone is always prepared. Everyone is always on time. We run things tight."

Then I asked the CEO, "Would you describe yourself as 'tight'?"

"Of course!" he said.

"Well, you were 10 minutes late to our last call, and the one before that you flat out missed," I reminded him.

"OK," he admitted sheepishly, "I'm not tight. That's why I need everyone else to be tight, to make up for me."

I appreciate what he was trying to do, and maybe you can see yourself in his story, but leadership doesn't work this way. If you ask your team to be on time, yet you are late, that creates an inherent distrust and disrespect. On top of that, it's unlikely they'll be on time. And it sure isn't leading by example.

One of the reasons leadership is so difficult is that you're held to a different standard. By virtue of your position, whenever you make a misstep, it's magnified a thousand times. If you're in a bad mood just one day, you may get labeled as grumpy. If you snap at someone, people will be on edge for weeks. If someone sees you giving someone a break and they don't know all the back story, they may think you're playing favorites.

You need to get your head around this fact as a leader. You're going to have to embody what you expect even *more* than what you expect from your team, if you want to be a highly effective leader. And you can start with your commitments.

With all that said, even with the best intentions, sometimes you won't be able to fulfill your commitments. For example, if you commit to working out for 30 minutes every day and then you break your arm; you promise to speak at a conference and later someone passes away and you want to attend the funeral; or the big project you're managing runs into an unexpected obstacle, you're likely going to miss your commitment, and you need to address it.

In cases like these, it's time to renegotiate the commitment. Renegotiation is when you contact whoever you made the agreement with, explain the situation and come up with an alternate plan. The most important aspects of renegotiating any commitment are:

- Do it in a timely manner. This means reaching out as soon as you know you won't be able to fulfill the commitment, or the deadline is in jeopardy. This does NOT mean you wait until after the deadline's been missed.
- Take full ownership and responsibility. Don't make excuses or blame others. Just lay out the facts, and if it's an issue you or your team should have known about or that you caused, own that.
- Have a suggested plan for what to do next. This puts everyone in a forward-looking mode instead of a "why did this happen" mindset and shows that you've thought about how to rectify things proactively.

When you follow these three steps you'll find that almost no one has an issue with the renegotiation, and they may even respect you for the way you've handled it. As long as whatever comes up wasn't for lack of trying or something you could have reasonably predicted, I don't think of a renegotiation as a failed commitment. It's just an adjustment to the original agreement.

A few other points about commitments:

- **A commitment should be something that can be either done or not done; if there's any grey area, it's not a commitment.**

On this basis, these are not commitments: *I'll call you soon. I'll get that to you by next week. I'll do a better job next time.*

These, on the other hand, are commitments: *I'll call you by 2:00 PM tomorrow. I'll make sure there are no grammar or math errors in the proposal next time. I'll get that to you by close of business next Wednesday.* (Note: Close of business means 5:00 PM in the time zone of the person you're committing to.)

- **Commitments made to ourselves are just as important as the ones we make to others.**

Remember, everything we're learning here can be applied to others as well as ourselves. In this case, we're referring to your internal commitments. How often have you heard about a good book and said to yourself, *Wow, I HAVE to read that book!* I could fill a room from top to bottom with all the books I told myself I have to read and never have. These are all failed internal agreements.

To tighten this up, make a simple change in your language so that what was an internal commitment becomes a statement. For example, say to yourself. *Hey, that looks like an interesting book. If I think of it, maybe I'll read it one day.* Or, *I'll put that book on my reading list.* In both statements, you acknowledge the book without creating a promise to yourself you probably won't keep. Remember, when you create agreements—with others and especially with yourself—and then don't keep them, it creates internal stress and saps your energy.

- **It's better to create far fewer commitments and keep them, than make more and keep fewer.**

As a leader, you have more on your plate than you know what to do with. By picking and choosing commitments, you're strengthening your integrity and spending more time on what's important. Instead of "Hey, good seeing you again, let's meet for coffee soon!" say "Hey. Good seeing you again."

Instead of "I have to lose that XX pounds," say "I'm going to work out at least once this week," or "I'm going to find an accountability group for getting in shape." Instead of "I'll get that to you tomorrow," say "I'll get that to you next week."

Instead of "I'll send you the name of that podcast/book/show," say "If you want the name of that and can't find it, send me an email." Save yourself from yet one more thing on your to-do list…

As you can probably tell, I put a lot of stock in commitments. I worked hard for a few months to get very strong in mine. As a member of Entrepreneurs Organization and later on the local board of directors, I got to interact with a lot of fellow business owners. One entrepreneur asked me to help coach him and his management team. During the first meeting, I explained that we would make commitments, be clear in them, and I expected that both he and I would follow through with what we promised. I told him I was very serious about this.

He said that he expected this because he'd heard about my stance on commitments from a few different people, and he was looking forward to it. Later, I reflected, *I have a reputation for making clear commitments and fulfilling them. I'm proud of that.*

What's YOUR reputation around commitments? Do people trust that if you say something you'll absolutely do it? Do you start meetings exactly on time? Do you do employee reviews when you're supposed to, without rescheduling them? Do you meet with customers, vendors, and partners as often as you agree to?

If your commitments aren't rock-solid, you have some work to do.

Exploration

Reflect on commitments you've made over the last few days to other people. Are they necessary and realistic? Are they specific?

How do you run meetings—do you start them on time or late? As a participant, are you early or late?

Now take some time to make commitments to yourself about your commitments and your integrity.

Creating A Culture of Trust

After getting clear on commitments for yourself, it's time to help your staff get very clear on theirs. All the same rules apply. Their commitments should be crystal clear. They should renegotiate when they can't fulfill them, and they should also be mindful of fulfilling their commitments to *their* team.

I've never seen a high-performing team that didn't have this focus on commitments. By requiring a team to have this level of integrity, you will shape a culture where people trust each other and devote themselves to following through on promises. It takes some time to build, but it's a joy to experience once it takes hold.

Being strong in your commitments is like a muscle—the more you do it, the better you'll get.

Here are two steps to follow to bring your team into more integrity:

1. Teach them about commitments and share your commitment to them.

Spend a meeting going through this chapter with your team. Have an open conversation. Ask them where you're soft with your commitments. Tell them to call you out when you slip, that you're fully on board with your commitments, and that you expect they'll get on board with theirs as well.

Ease into things gradually. If this is somewhat new, give people (and yourself) some grace at the beginning, and slowly tighten up. For example, if someone starts a meeting late, gently mention it to them when you're one-on-one. If they do it again within a week or two, then mention it in the meeting in front of others.

2. Create a process in your weekly and monthly meetings.

Here's a system called the Self-Reporting Accountability Cycle, or SRAC (Figure 19: Self-Reporting Accountability Cycle), that's easy to implement and teaches people to take ownership for themselves.

For regular meetings, at the end of each meeting, review and take note of the commitments that come up. Put a name beside each commitment, along with the due date.

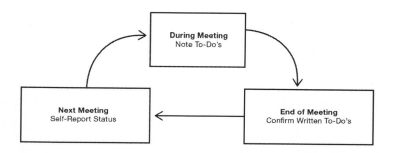

Figure 19: Self-Reporting Accountability Cycle

At the beginning of the next meeting, pull up the list of commitments and have each person self-report whether they got theirs done or not. They should only say a YES or a NO and then whoever is keeping track should mark that down. This eliminates excuses, however if they've renegotiated before the meeting, that's OK.

This process takes all the pressure off of you holding them accountable. When people have to self-report in front of their peers, it's very obvious who's performing and who's not. No one wants to tell the whole team that they don't have their tasks done, especially multiple weeks in a row.

Sometimes a leader comes to me for coaching who feels like they're just barely keeping up with life. Let's call them Sonya. Sonya is stressed out beyond belief. It's like she's lost all sense of control in her role, the pressure is all-consuming, and she's struggling to make it from one day to the next.

Our first session consists of Sonya giving me a huge list of everything that's going on, which is exhausting just to listen to. Each day is taken up with fighting fires and there's no progress on the true issues. Her mental health is suffering. She's slipping into bad habits (binge eating, alcohol, drugs, other addictions and distractions). She doesn't have a clue where to start to get back on track.

You may be interested to know that with a person like Sonya, the first thing I have her start to do is commit to one single, simple thing between now and the next session.

"No," she exclaims, "I need to do more."

I explain, "Sonya, right now you need to regain your sense of self, to re-establish your relationship with yourself. And you need to do that by making and completing commitments with yourself."

She fights me for a while on it, but I hold fast and in the end we make a super-simple commitment. Something like, "Go to bed before 9 PM three out of the next seven nights."

Every single time the client fails to fulfill the commitment.

Sonya has been stuck solving so many crises that she's lost the ability to work strategically. It's like she's stuck in flight/flight/freeze mode and needs a reset to get back to being the leader she needs to be. That's why the Sonyas of the world inevitably come back and say, "Well I got to bed at 9 for two nights, then the third night I got to bed at 9:30. That counts, right? After all, I was close." No, that doesn't count. On some level Sonya's ego is trying to be crafty and get by without fulfilling the commitment.

I explain that she's failed and we go through her life to see where else she's not fulfilling her commitments. And just as importantly, we look at *where other people are not fulfilling their commitments to Sonya.*

These initial coaching sessions are always eye-opening, and like I said, they happen this way every single time. It's like the client's ego wants to test to see if it can *almost* fulfill the commitment and talk its way out of it. At the end of the session, we set another simple commitment, and that one they fulfill. We talk about how that feels. Of course, it feels good, and they feel their strength returning.

Next, we set two commitments before meeting again, then three, so that their commitment muscle starts getting strong and toned again. And with that, Sonya's back to her old self—actually, an upgraded version of her old self—and back to changing the world.

When you have someone on your team that's super stressed out, and lost their sense of control, try the above process. Coach them to follow through on a simple commitment, one at a time, and go from there. This process goes a long way when you need to lead others.

Everything starts and ends with commitments. If you value integrity, start by giving your word and making good on it. From there you build trust, respect, and loyalty, creating the type of relationships that will provide dividends for the rest of your life.

Exploration

How would you rate your team on commitments overall? Do people give deadlines and miss them regularly? Do some people do that more than others?

What's your plan, for either your whole team and / or individuals, to create a culture where everyone commits and follows through every time?

CHAPTER 25:

The 4 Growth Leadership Styles

How many people in your life do you lack a genuine connection with? What about the people who report to you, or people on your Senior Leadership team? Are any of them hard to understand, and would it be helpful if you had a magic formula to figure them out?

Human beings are not all wired the same. When we forget that, we try to force everyone to be mirror images of ourselves—and get confused and frustrated when they aren't. However, when we can identify how people are wired, and relate to them as who they really are, a whole new world of leadership effectiveness opens up.

To help you do that, I've developed four leadership types—loosely based on William Moulton Marston's DISC model of behavior—that can help you navigate your leadership journey. By getting to grips with the characteristics of each type, you'll understand yourself better—what drives you, your strengths, where your blind spots are—and also help you work with others.

Here's a link to the free Growth Leadership Style Assessment so you can quickly find your own style: RMichaelAnderson.com/LeadershipQuiz (QR code included)

(Most people finish the assessment in under 5 minutes.)

If you're not in a position to take the assessment right now, just focus on reading through the descriptions of the types.

Every leader fits within one of four types shown below (Figure 20). Some people may sit closer to the middle, meaning they're more balanced, and some near the edge, meaning they exhibit more of that particular trait. Leaders can be a blend of two different types, meaning they are near the separator line and embody traits from two different styles. People also may embody different types in different parts of their life; for example in someone's family life they display the behaviors of one type, and another type when it comes to work.

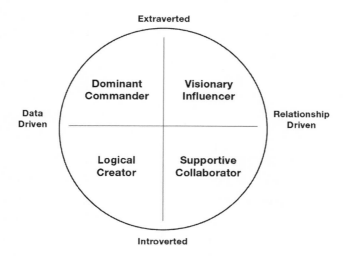

Figure 20: The Four Types of Leaders

Type 1: Dominant Commanders

In the top left quadrant, we have the Dominant Commanders. These individuals have a lot of natural self-confidence and drive, stemming from their desire to win. They are very competitive and prefer to lead rather than to follow. This means they frequently find themselves in leadership and management positions.

Many times, Dominant Commanders get frustrated with people they perceive as less driven to win, or in the different ways. They have huge expectations for themselves and hate to be controlled by others. They also tend to lack patience, take lots of risks, and are decisive. This means sometimes they win big, and other times they move forward too quickly and get in trouble. If you are a Dominant Commander, the good news is you're a natural leader and you have a lot of positive attributes that will support a great career; you're driven, focused, and strong.

To level up, address your blind spots:

- Develop your patience. Make sure you meditate and take some time away from work. You can easily overwork and burn out.
- Work on delegating and empowering or supporting others. While you probably can do most jobs, you won't get where you want unless you build a loyal, competent team.
- Don't always challenge authority and presume you know better. Get mentors, and ask for help sometimes.
- Some people, especially people who aren't very aggressive or outspoken, may be intimidated by you, and therefore resent you, so be aware of this. Identify who those people are and get them on your side by slowing down and talking to them one-on-one.
- Learn how to play the long game. Winning long-term means being strategic and patient. Give up small victories from time to time in order to build trust and respect.

When it comes to your team, you'll know someone's a Dominant Commander when:

- They speak in short, direct, sometimes brash sentences.
- They always want to get right to the point.
- They seem to have a temper or get bored easily.
- They are consumed by winning, coming in first, and getting ahead.
- They piss people off and don't seem to care.

When working with a Dominant Commander:

- Get right to the point. Time is money. They HATE small talk. You can go into their office and launch right into whatever you're there for. Not only will they not mind, they'll appreciate it.
- You can challenge them. This earns their respect and they'll often love it—just be prepared to back it up and get challenged back.
- Understand that they will move quickly, especially when there's a clear benefit. When you present something to them, give a short summary with a clear ROI, and a way to move forward immediately. Be ready to field a few questions, which you can give short answers to, i.e. "Yes" or "No." If they see how it will help them win and get ahead, they'll commit to get the job done right then and there.

Type 2: Visionary Influencers

In the top right quadrant, we have the Visionary Influencers—the fun ones. These are the big thinkers who love to laugh, talk to everyone, and have a lot of friends. They often find a home in the marketing or creative side of the business, and they're driven by a sense of belonging, status, and being liked.

Usually natural extroverts, Visionary Influencers love the spotlight, are good at public speaking and present themselves well. They treasure relationships and do not enjoy repetition or details. If you're a Visionary Influencer, the good news is, you're very likeable, great at networking and developing relationships. You're also a high-level and strategic thinker, and because of these traits, people like to follow you.

To level up, address your blind spots:

- You often reach higher-level positions through your drive, strategic outlook, and relationships. But because Visionary Influencers are so concerned with what other people think, they suffer from more imposter syndrome than other types. Be aware of this and develop your self-esteem so you aren't so reliant on other people's perceived views of you.

- You hate details, so develop systems that prevent you from being constantly late, missing deadlines, and letting people down (which really bothers you even though it happens often.) You have a fear of missing out, so you have the tendency to say "yes" to everything. Be aware of how full your plate is already.

- Being a leader means you're not always friends with everyone. Difficult conversations, confrontation, and delivering bad news are things you probably put off when you should address them head-on.

- Make sure you aren't talking too much during meetings.

- You love collaborating and being around people, so make sure your role has plenty of this built in. Don't take on projects that have you working alone for extended periods of time.

- When working with more logical, analytical people, your communication may be too high-level and aspirational for them. Make sure you slow down and listen to them, address their concerns, and get them on board with your ideas, otherwise they won't buy in.

You'll know someone's a Visionary Influencer when:

- They speak loudly, talk a lot, and use a lot of gestures.
- They jump at the chance to talk in front of others.
- They have grand, forward-thinking, sweeping, visionary plans.
- They love social occasions, meeting for long lunches, and getting to know people personally.
- They have a lot of friends and are always surrounded by people.

When working with a Visionary Influencer:

- Paint a big, grand picture. Show them how what you're proposing fits into their vision.
- Avoid talking about details and don't make them responsible for details in a project.
- Show them how what you're trying to do will make them look cool, give them status, and make people look up to them.
- Talk about how FUN everything will be and how much they will enjoy it.

Type 3: Logical Creators

In the bottom left, we have the Logical Creators, the analytical leader type. While they often come from the finance or accounting department, in certain cases they are excellent salespeople and creative people because they've learned how to successfully follow a process. They are driven by doing an excellent job, especially when it comes to complex tasks. Precise, accurate, and detail oriented, they like to complete projects for the reward of a job done right—sometimes sacrificing speed or budget. They often will take on a complex project as a personal challenge and do whatever's in their power to make it succeed.

Logical Creators thrive when they can work alone and often are naturally introverted. They also excel at strategic planning, managing projects, and are very reliable. Because they think through consequences thoroughly they can often find potential risks and problems at an early stage.

If you are a Logical Creator, you understand how systems, business, products, and more all work together. However, the people and relationship parts of leadership don't come as naturally to you.

To level up, address your blind spots:

- With leadership comes risk, responsibility, and a lot of fast decisions. Learn how to commit to a decision with incomplete information, and be OK with things not being perfect.
- Your focus and seriousness may be misunderstood by some people. It is good to show some personality from time to time, and remember that other people may be more sensitive than you are.
- People are a valuable resource. You need to invest time in your relationships to get the best out of them.
- When you're working with someone who has big, grand plans, don't always press them for details. Sometimes they're just talking about possibilities, and you can come across as negative when you ask for specifics too soon.

You know someone's a Logical Creator when:

- They generally talk with a monotonous voice without much variation.
- They want to see the details and understand all aspects of things.
- They find risks and potential problems.
- They seemingly only make a decision when they have all the information.

When working with a Logical Creator:

- Give them all the information they need to make a decision. Don't rush them or try to shorten their decision-making process if you don't have to.
- Address any risks upfront when presenting any proposals.
- Make sure you position them to succeed; groups and collaboration, a lot of personal interaction, and even public presentations may not be natural or comfortable for them.

Type 4: Supportive Collaborators

Often the glue of an office or team, in our final quadrant, we have the Supportive Collaborators. These individuals love working in the background to make sure everyone's happy and effective. Their driver is harmony; when everyone's getting along and the team is performing well, they're at their happiest. Supportive Collaborators often come from somewhere in operations or a support role.

While leadership is not natural to Supportive Collaborators—they're used to working from the back—the ones who learn what it takes can become fantastic leaders. These are the unsung heroes. If they're bought into the company, team, or leader, they'll do almost anything—and morph into whoever they need to become—in order to protect and serve.

However, within a team, Supportive Collaborators avoid the spotlight, do a great job in their own area, and keep any eye on everyone else to see who else they can support. The team probably leans on them; individuals likely go to them when they need someone to talk to because they're a great listener. They may not get the kudos they've earned because they are so focused on being of service.

If you're a Supportive Collaborator, you probably have a great track record and many supporters. You care deeply about the team and having everyone succeed.

To level up, address your blind spots:

- You love comfort and routine, so stretch yourself to get used to change.
- Confrontation and difficult conversations give you a lot of anxiety but with focus, you'll learn how to handle them.
- It's natural for people to do some self-promotion. Look for areas where you can speak more in meetings and actively participate more.
- Learn how to be more strategic. (We'll get to that later in this book.)
- Learn how to set clear, self-supporting boundaries. Be wary of getting bullied or taken advantage of because you're nice and want harmony.

You know someone's a Supportive Collaborator when:

- They generally speak fairly softly.
- They may not participate as much in larger meetings but will share their concerns in a private setting.
- They don't draw attention to themselves.

When working with a Supportive Collaborator:

- Show them that whatever you're proposing will make everyone's life better. They may be worried about the happiness of entry-level people; make sure you hear their concerns with compassion
- Supportive Collaborators often have the ear of high-level people, so never discount them. If you can get them bought in, they can be instrumental in influencing others on the team.
- To find out what they're really thinking, you may need to create a safe, one-on-one space before they'll speak openly.
- If you're brash or loud, you may intimidate them. Keep this in mind when interacting with them.

You can see the potential in identifying someone's type, then adapting how you communicate with them. When someone comes to me with problems relating to a co-worker, we go through the process of identifying their type. That often sheds new light on how they can get the relationship back on track.

Exploration

Think of two or three people you work the most with. What type do you think they are? Taking that into account, how can you adjust working with them so you can have a more effective relationship?

What are three ways you can amplify your strengths and work on your blind spots?

If you took the assessment online you received a description. How well does it fit with your sense of self? If you haven't taken the assessment, remember you can do it here: <u>RMichaelAnderson.com/LeadershipQuiz</u>

CHAPTER 26:

Lasting Employee Engagement

In 1914, Sir Ernest Shackleton [28] had a plan to achieve the first land crossing of the Antarctic, starting from Britain via Argentina on his ship the Endurance. The astonishing story that follows is a brilliant illustration of team engagement.

First, let's put ourselves in Shackleton's shoes and keep in mind that in those days there were no long-range radios, North Face jackets, or portable heaters for him or his crew of 27 men, most of who were inexperienced and new to Arctic journeys. Due to the worst weather in recorded history, the expedition went very poorly—to say the least. Six weeks in, the ship got stuck in ice, and one of the crew described it as "frozen like an almond in the middle of a chocolate bar." They were stuck there for 10 months, sleeping in tents made from ripped sails and hunting seals and penguins to survive. When the ice finally shifted, the Endurance was ripped to pieces and sunk, forcing them to turn to lifeboats and sleds.

Shackleton led his team across the ice, covering about a mile a day for months. Then, when circumstances finally allowed and after three failed attempts, he was able to rescue his crew, bringing every single member home alive.

---

28   The whole expedition is captured in an amazing book Endurance: Shackleton's Incredible Voyage to the Antarctic by Alfred Lansing.

There are a few leadership lessons from how Shackleton kept his party together.

First, he always modeled hope and optimism.

As a leader, Shackleton knew that if he showed any hint of doubt about a good outcome, it would doom his entire crew. Although he had his own personal down moments, he kept them to himself.

Second, he created tangible ways to keep people's spirits up.

While there were periods of intense work, the majority of time consisted of sitting around in the freezing cold with nothing to do. So, they manufactured ways to keep busy. They celebrated birthdays and anniversaries. They had competitions. They found activities to rally around. Anything to keep their minds off the adverse conditions.

When people started to crack, he would buddy them up with someone in a stronger mindset with the instructions to keep each other sane. He knew that if one person lost faith, others would quickly follow.

Finally, he had a clear vision.

Shackleton told his crew that he would get them home; he believed that in his soul, and he kept reminding them of that.

While none of us will run into anything this dramatic when looking to motivate our teams (I hope), it shows us that the leadership strategies we're learning are timeless and powerful, and we can aspire to be even a little bit like the leader Shackleton was.

You won't have to lead them across the Antarctic, but do you know what actually motivates employees? When I pose this question to leaders, the most common answers are: promotions, money or compensation, praise, and title. And yes, these external things do motivate people for a short period of time—usually up to a three-month period, but often less.

This means if you give someone a raise to motivate them, they'll likely be more engaged for a few months before the newness wears off. Then you'll be stuck wondering how to motivate them again, or giving them raise after raise and promotion after promotion until the situation is unsustainable.

What Daniel Pink teaches us in his excellent book *Drive_: The Surprising Truth About What Motivates Us* is that there are three long-term motivators: mastery, autonomy, and purpose. In other words, people want to do their job, they want to do it really well, they want to be trusted to do it their way, and they want to do it in service to a purpose.

We won't go into mastery and autonomy in this book as they fall more into the training, development, and management disciplines. What we will focus on is giving people a purpose. There's a good chance you've thought about purpose before, so take a moment now and consider: what is your company or team's purpose? Is it inspiring, simple and exciting? Do the values and desires of your employees align with it?

If you answered yes to all those questions, great job—feel free to skip this chapter unless you think you can improve your answers. If you stumbled over your answers, this chapter will be both valuable and important.

Every business should have what I call "Guiding Principles" which can include a few different components, most often a Purpose Statement, Vision Statement, and a set of Core Values. Let's touch on each of these briefly so you understand what they are and why they're important.

Core Values

Think of Core Values as the DNA of your company. Are you risk takers? Or does your focus center on providing safety and consistency for your customers? Risk-taking and safety are two examples of core values that happen to be opposites; notice that if you try to have both, it will cause confusion and disconnection. You and your company can't be everything to everyone, and your values are an opportunity to get clear about who you are to people both internal and external to your organization.

One reason companies have core values is to attract people in line with those values. People who aren't aligned with them won't join or do business with your company.

Meta, the parent company of Facebook, is well known for its "hacker culture." While hacking is not a stated core value, it's part of their DNA. A good question Meta could ask in a job interview is, "Tell me about a time when you've hacked something." A core value of Amazon is frugality. That means if you like flying business class and having a company expense account, you probably don't want to work there.

Many companies aspire to having "fun" as a core value. That may or may not be true for your company. For example, even though we won recognition for being the number one best place to work in San Diego[29], no one there would have described my company as fun. We implemented accounting software. Most of us were introverted and on the quiet, bookish side. But people loved working there; most, if not everyone enjoyed their job. Employees got to be personal friends with other employees. More so than "fun" the value that was in our DNA was a deep desire to help companies by automating their processes, and find efficient, creative ways to do

---

29   Best places to work awards. San Diego Business Journal. (2014). https://www.cbjonline.com/a3sdbj/resources/supplements/PDF/20140818_BPW.pdf

so. (I know that that sounds nerdy, but it's true and a real part of our success.)

Have a closer look at whether "fun" is really a core value or whether it's your ego that wants that.

Do you think "honesty" or "integrity" is a core value of your company? If so, does anyone ever start a meeting late—and if they do, is that breaking one of your values? Would these core values extend to someone having a frank, honest conversation with someone when they have an issue? If not, in order to uphold the core values of honesty and integrity, you may need a framework for how that's carried out in real-life, otherwise the misalignment could cause problems.

Questions like these demonstrate why it's important to develop a Values Handbook that outlines how a company's core values will be carried out. As a leader, your life gets so much easier when you have a team that shares the same values. You can readily motivate and encourage them, there is trust inherent in your interactions, and the common values result in a sense of connection and belonging.

Here's the catch: remember the story of the CEO who wanted to have a core value of "tight" when he didn't embody that value himself? As a leader, your values have to be an authentic reflection of you, and you have to set an example when it comes to each of them. Even small slip ups that go unaddressed can send the message that the company values aren't important. But when you do commit to the company values, and your team sees you living them every day, it creates trust, loyalty, and a bond that lasts through thick and thin.

Exploration

Make a list of 5 to 10 words or phrases that you think describe your company. Have your leadership team do the same.

Now, spend time comparing and discussing what you each came up with. What's the same? What are the differences? Why are they different?

Vision Statement

When you're about to step on a bus, there's one critical piece of information you absolutely want: where is the bus going?

As a leader, you need to know where you're taking your team. And just the same, *they* want to know where you're taking them. In your mind, you have an idea of how your team and the area you're responsible for will look in a month, a year, or five years. What's important is to get clear on that and communicate it to everyone involved.

A vision doesn't even have to be achievable. The vision for The Alzheimer's Association is "A world without Alzheimer's and all other dementia." Is that even possible? Probably not. But if someone close to you dies or experiences Alzheimer's or dementia, or you work in those fields, you'd get energized by that vision.

In 1980, a young Bill Gates told the world his vision for Microsoft: "A microcomputer on every desk and in every home running Microsoft software." While many doubted him, he came very close to achieving it.

Just like with Core Values, some people will hear your vision and get excited. It will inspire them and they'll work through difficulties and chaos because they want to be part of the finished product. Also likely, a few people won't be on board with your vision. But isn't it better to know that now, rather than after they join up and become a disgruntled, negative employee?

Your vision will be of interest not only to your team, but also your boss, investors, and even your peers. It may even help attract and retain key customers and strengthen your relationships with partners and vendors.

Exploration

Do you have a vision of what your company will look like in the future? If not, start crafting one. Make sure it's inspiring and powerful.

If you already have one, or you're in the process of coming up with one, practice telling people about it. Be sure to put your passion and enthusiasm into it. If you don't get excited about it, no one else will.

Purpose Statement

Have you ever volunteered your time for a cause? Did you feel cheated out of that time because you weren't paid? Or did you feel that the time was well spent because it supported something you believe in? Even if the work was difficult, it likely flowed and was fulfilling, because you believed in the purpose of the project or organization. Your effort helped—was in service—to someone or something else.

The last, most important and sometimes most difficult Guiding Principle is to have a clear purpose. This is what gets you out of bed happy and makes you enjoy work every day. Now if you read that last sentence and thought *I struggle to get out of bed and I loathe my work,* then you either need to find fresh purpose where you are, or, find somewhere more aligned to work.

Here's the difficult part of solving the purpose equation: it can't be about making money, being number one in your industry, or anything else to do with the company's success. That's because no one gets excited about the company making more money, and while there may be pride in seeing the company grow and thrive, helping a company gain market share isn't a huge driver in the lives of most of your employees.

A friend of mine, Drew Louis, owns Del Toro Loan Servicing. When investors make loans to others, Del Toro processes these, so they help with the setup, send out statements, and so on. Drew was having issues with his company. His employees weren't very engaged, there was high turnover, and growth was stalling. People just weren't that excited about coming into work every day and helping to process loans.

When Drew began searching for a solution to these problems, he found that on a deep level he was of great service to his customers. The people who were taking out loans through his company were sending their kids to college, buying their dream home, and taking vacations they'd been planning for years. None of these things would have been possible without their services. What it boiled down to was this: Drew's company was giving these customers *freedom*. And that's exciting.

Drew embraced this idea and made it part of his company's DNA. He got clear on the value his company was delivering and embedded it into everything they did. The attitude of service, of helping people manifest what they wanted in their lives, began to infuse all the processes that kept the company going, all the interactions between team members and clients.

People who didn't get it left the company. New people were added only if they got excited about the mission of the company—being of service. The result? Turnover dropped and revenue, profits, and customer satisfaction all skyrocketed. All this cost Drew zero money; it simply took a shift in mindset about the company's purpose.

But, what do you do if you run a team and don't have much say in your company's values, vision, or purpose? Or, perhaps the company doesn't seem to take these very seriously? You need to have values, vision, and purpose for your team. Just because your company isn't giving you what you need isn't an excuse. And the guiding principles for the company may not accurately reflect what your team needs.

The values, vision, and purpose for an accounting department probably won't be the same as the marketing or sales department. That's OK—they have different functions. As a team leader or manager, it's up to you to develop these, even if you only develop them for yourself to guide you in your own role.

Taking this to the next level, you can develop guiding principles for your personal life. What do you want your life to look like? What is your purpose and what are your values? Figuring these out is an impactful exercise that can bring you clarity, focus, easier decision-making, and success on your terms.

Exploration

Why does your company exist, outside of making a profit?

Why do you do what you do, instead of something else? Why do other people enjoy your industry and your company?

Developing and implementing these guiding principles—Core Values, Vision and Purpose—takes time. I estimate it took my company five years from the time I learned about them and decided to utilize them, to having them fully implemented. Even so, it was one of the best investments I've ever made, and it's something you'll need in order to develop your competitive differentiation, to create a high-performance culture, and to facilitate growth.

If you see the benefit of this work and want assistance developing and integrating your guiding principles, drop me a line—my team and I can help michael@RMichaelAnderson.com.

CHAPTER 27:

Team-Level Ownership

As we covered in an earlier chapter on the Owner versus Victim choice, getting clear about what you can and can't control—and releasing any victim mentality—puts you in an incredibly powerful place as a leader. Now, can you imagine if everyone on your team, or everyone in your company, was fully focused on taking ownership in every situation? You would be unstoppable.

To get to that place, first and foremost you have to embody taking ownership yourself. As I've said previously, people are going to mirror how you show up. Once you've committed to the shift from victim to owner yourself, it's time to coach others on adopting the same mindset.

The next time you catch someone complaining, blaming, or otherwise playing the victim, there are several questions you can ask them to change their thought process:

I hear you, but what can you do to solve the problem?

I know it's hard. What's your next step?

If you want assistance figuring out a solution, I'm here to help.

Playing the victim doesn't just happen on a person-by-person basis. It can extend into teams, divisions, and even whole companies.

At one of my previous companies, 95% of our revenue came from reselling and servicing a Microsoft ERP (accounting, distribution and manufacturing) product. Microsoft is a big company, and everyone on my team would complain about Microsoft, from the product to marketing to sales and support. In other words, my entire company was playing victim to the Microsoft relationship. We had a culture of victimhood around our Microsoft relationship.

I had an executive coach, Michelle, who was working with me and the management team and she called us out on it. "Your whole company complains about Microsoft a lot. Why don't you switch products?" I replied, "They make the best product of this type for my market. It's very complex business to business software so there are always issues, but we found Microsoft to be the best choice overall."

Michelle said, "From an outsider's point of view, it all comes across as very negative. You might want to consider not complaining about them so much." I understood what she was talking about and worked with her on how to reverse the trend. This is what I told our staff:

"I want to bring something up. I noticed I've been complaining about Microsoft a lot and I hear others doing the same. I want to shift that. It's not helping anything, and it puts us in a victimhood mindset. I'm going to challenge all of us to start speaking positively about Microsoft. Because at the end of the day, they're the best product out there, and in their own way they do take care of us.

"Starting now, I'm only going to talk positively about them. I might slip up because I've been doing this complaining for years, so if you catch me, I want you to let me know. And I'm going to do the same with everybody else. Can we agree on that?"

I got a "Yes" from the group—but the real test would be how well we executed on it.

Over the next couple of weeks, whenever I would forget and slip back into my critical ways, they'd call me out. "Mike, you said you wouldn't do that." I'd thank them while taking complete ownership. "Ah, you're totally right! My bad. Thanks for reminding me."

Once they saw that I was committed, and that I was thankful and open when they reminded me, they started to change. Over the next few weeks how we talked about Microsoft shifted—and it seemed like our relationship with them also changed. We got more leads, it appeared that we got better service, and it felt like everything worked more smoothly from then on.

The victimhood mentality can creep up anywhere. Internally, sales often complains about marketing, and accounting seems to always moan that no one turns in their expense account on time, and so on. The sooner you can identify victimhood on the team or at the organizational level, the sooner you can shift the mindset back to ownership, and the more happy and successful everyone will be.

Exploration

Who on your team plays the victim? How can you coach them to shift into ownership?

Are there any groups in your company who play the victim? How can you help them realize this and shift into ownership?

It's critical that you coach people who are playing the victim into taking ownership as soon as it creeps in. This may even mean having a one-on-one with them and telling them bluntly that their mindset needs to change; and one step further, by letting go of someone who stays stuck in victimhood.

CHAPTER 28:

Letting People Go

Part of leading others is doing the tough stuff, including the delicate art of firing people. In all my years in business, from working my way up the corporate ladder to running my own businesses, and coaching leaders around the world, I can honestly say that people should be fired a lot more often—and a lot more quickly.

Time after time, employees who are disgruntled, a horrible fit and even unethical stay in their roles because the leader doesn't have the courage to show them the door. This isn't me being harsh. Being harsh is keeping someone on your team who isn't enjoying themselves, isn't doing their job well, and most of all is bringing others down.

Don't get me wrong, if someone isn't performing or living up to the standards, values, or culture you're building, first try to coach, support, and mentor them. If they're interested in changing, apply themselves, and show a measurable difference in their attitude or performance, then you're not only on the right track—you've shown them that you'll invest in them and have strengthened your relationship.

But if they're not keen on coaching, don't make steps to change, and their performance stays the same, you need to help them find their way off your team—whether that's finding another team within the company for them to join, or simply firing them. I've found that people either change quickly or don't change much at all. If they don't start to "get it" fairly fast, more coaching or waiting longer usually doesn't work. In fact, you're probably delaying in order to avoid the problem.

If a high-performing team is your goal, you need to be firm in your standards for everyone who works within it. If you have someone who's not living up to what's needed, make sure you first work with your HR department to make sure they get the chance that they deserve, and that you're legally covered to make the transition properly if things don't pan out.

Leaders hate to fire people and they come up with all sorts of rationalizations for why they should make do with poor performance—all so they don't have to let someone go. That's certainly the case for me. Firing people is one of the tasks I like least, even though it's so necessary.

In one study, retired CEOs were asked what they'd do differently as a leader and manager if they had the chance. There were two answers that were the most common, by far: First, they would lay people off faster in a downturn. While that's a difficult task, nothing drains cash flow more than keeping people around for too long, and that liquidity is especially important when things get slow.

Second, when the retired CEOs looked back on their careers, they said they'd let go of mediocre employees faster, so they could replace them with high-performers and create a high-performing culture.

If you catch yourself getting stuck around firing people and not pulling the trigger, bookmark this chapter and come back to it. I work with a lot of leaders who need an extra push in this area.

With support, the big move to clear someone out will feel positive, especially when a much better person comes on board.

As the leader, one of your main tasks is to develop a high-performing team. This means that each and every person needs the right skillset, the right attitude and the ability to perform. If they don't, then it's your job to rectify it.

Think about it: when you keep someone on who's not pulling their weight, what kind of message do you think it sends to your A players? You're telling them that you accept mediocrity and that the A players don't have to perform at a high level.

The high performers will start to resent this person, and eventually you, for allowing this to happen. Then they'll lose respect for you and ultimately leave for a team where they can be surrounded by other superstars, and challenged to grow. All of a sudden your hesitancy to let go of a mediocre team member is costing you your A team.

If you know you have to let someone go and you're procrastinating, here are a few points to keep in mind:

- It's almost never as bad as you think it's going to be.

  I was on the phone with a business owner who knew he had to fire a project manager. But he'd been resisting it for weeks and still hadn't made the move. I told him to go do it right now and call me back.

  Five minutes later, he called and told me she'd been expecting it. It was a smooth, quick conversation. Turns out he'd spent weeks stressing about it...and the whole time she knew it was coming.

- The person will be happier somewhere else.

  If they aren't performing on your team, chances are they aren't happy. People want to be good at their job. If they're struggling at your firm or on your team, it isn't fun for them. Once you let them go, there's a 99% chance that they'll land on their feet in a week or two and hardly ever think of you or your company again.

- You're going to be incredibly happy when it's done.

After you have the difficult conversation, you'll feel like a weight's been lifted off of you. You probably aren't aware of how much background stress it's causing in your subconscious. Pull the trigger and free yourself.

- Other people will be happier as well.

When you let go of someone who's muddling along, often you'll get positive, unexpected feedback from the rest of the team. People will let you know that they didn't get along with the person you let go, and that the person wasn't doing such a good job. If the person you fired worked with customers, you'll often find out the customer is happy they've moved on as well.

Of course, make sure you have a plan to handle things both externally (i.e. who's going to replace them on the project?) and internally (i.e. who's going to pick up this person's responsibilities, at least until you can bring someone else in?).

You'll ask yourself *why haven't I heard this feedback sooner?* People don't like to complain about or "tell on" others, so they ignore the person, assuming leadership—you— know what you're doing. But once the person's been let go, these people will come out of the woodwork to tell you what they've been thinking all along, which validates your decision.

- You'll find someone much better.

  I was feeling down one day after my COO quit. I was worried about the extra pressure her leaving would put on me and the team, and thought we'd lost an amazing person. While she did do a good job, after she left I started to see some of the holes in her performance, and realized that all wasn't as rosy as I thought (see above).

  Then one of my mentors told me, "Michael, whenever I lose a key employee, I always seem to find someone better." That was helpful for me, and I set the intention to bring someone in who was more effective than the last person. Not only did this help my mental health, it encouraged me to hold strong in my search until I did find the right person.

- Do it RIGHT AWAY—if it's cleared with HR.

  Once you double check with your HR department that you're cleared to let the person go, do it right away. Don't worry if it's a Monday or a Friday, or if it's before a holiday. Because once you do it, it will be OVER, you'll feel much freer, and YOUR energy will be cleared up.

- Here's how to handle the actual firing conversation.

  We'll go deeper into difficult conversations as a whole in a few chapters. But for now, if you have to let someone go—get right to the point, focus on facts, don't make anything personal, and be direct and firm.

  It's not a discussion; you're letting them know this is a decision that you've made. It will almost always be a short conversation. Let them know all the specific next steps, like their final compensation, what they need to turn in, what they can expect from HR, etc.

If the situation calls for it, make sure that right before you talk to them you shut off their access and email, and if they're in the office, make sure you or someone else is there as they empty their desk and escort them out. That may sound cold-hearted, but you don't want them to do anything stupid (like steal something) because they're hurt. That will cause issues for everyone for weeks or months.

I once hired a technical person for a much-needed position— someone I thought was going to be an excellent pick. He had all the certifications in the world, everyone at the company liked him immediately, and we couldn't wait for him to get up to speed.

As he got familiar with the product, he shared how he loved the company culture and would actively participate in meetings, help others out, and go every extra mile he could. However…when he started working on customer projects, things just didn't come together. He over-analyzed everything. What would take one developer 100 hours he would quote 500 for. We worked with him. We coached him. We had our CTO mentor him. Over a period of months, we did everything we could to help him succeed, but things never clicked for us and I had to let him go. I was sad and it was difficult. But it needed to be done.

I hope he's found a place where he's thriving and happy.

As for us, we found someone with fewer qualifications, but a knack for getting things done. He was coachable, took to learning very quickly, and ended up being one of our top performers.

Exploration

If you're in the position of needing to let someone go right now, shut this book, call your HR contact, then reach out to the person in question and DO IT NOW. You'll be happier for it, your team will be happier for it, and your customers will be happier for it. And, it's an act of compassion for them. You're freeing them up to find a better place, whatever that may be for them.

Soon, you'll be past the whole situation, and the person you let go will most likely be getting a new job, one that they'll enjoy a lot more.

This is your job as a leader; suck it up and get it done. You got this.

CHAPTER 29:

Difficult Conversations

The ability to initiate and handle difficult conversations is one of the most important skills a leader can have. Success here is the culmination of many of the different mindset skills we've covered in this book. And while there's no way to guarantee the result of a conversation, there's a lot you can do to influence it.

Here's a four-step Conversation Roadmap (Figure 21) that not only works for challenging conversations, but all discussions:

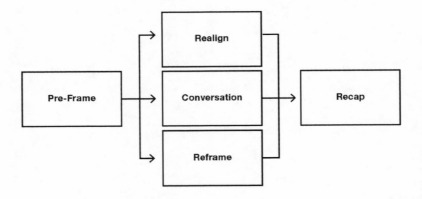

Figure 21: The Conversation Roadmap

Step 1: Pre-frame

The "framing effect," developed by two psychologists, Daniel Kahneman and Amos Tversky, describes a cognitive bias that people have when choosing from a set of options. It turns out that people make choices based more on *how information is worded* than the information itself. What this means is that what people experience is affected by everything that surrounds it, and when you understand that, you can create conversations that go well even when they're challenging.

Here's an example of the framing effect:

It's really hot out and you just walked two miles. Someone offers you an ice cream cone and you gladly eat it. A week later, you go to the doctor and they tell you that you have early onset diabetes. They then offer you an ice cream cone and this time you refuse it.

In both scenarios, you're offered an ice cream cone, but because of the different environments you were in, you made different choices. You can think of the doctor's office and the news of diabetes as the environment, or "frame" that influenced your choice to say no.

In a more practical example, an insurance salesperson may tell you the statistics about people passing away at your age, and then tell you a sad story about someone who didn't have insurance before pitching their product. The statistics and story are the frame that shapes your decision-making.

Here are two examples of pre-frames:

Let's say you're doing an employee review, and as part of that you look over the feedback you've received from the rest of the team. That information provides the frame for the rest of the performance review.

Or, perhaps you're at a yearly strategy meeting. At the beginning of the meeting, you review the previous year's strategy and performance so everyone has that in mind when setting a new direction for coming year. Last year's strategy is the pre-frame for discussing this year's. When it comes to specific discussions, always create a "pre-frame."

Here's a more detailed scenario of a pre-frame which we will use in each of the following steps to demonstrate how they apply:

Imagine someone who reports to you who is young and unpolished, though very hard-working and intelligent. You know their goal is to get promoted and they've shown that they're willing to learn and grow in order to get there. However, they're consistently late to work and to meetings.

You decide it's time to say something to them. Your first instinct is to let them know that you want to have a meeting with them about being late. But if you do that, you wonder how they'll show up in the meeting—will they be open and ready to hear your feedback, or will they be defensive and shut down? Most likely, hearing that the meeting is about their lateness, the team member will shift to their ego and will be defensive before the meeting even starts.

As you've learned, it's difficult to have a productive conversation with someone who's in their ego. Your job as leader is to support your team member to be in their authentic self, to stay connected, open, and engaged, so you think through the psychology and neuroscience of the situation and request the meeting as a chance to "review ways you can improve your chances for a promotion."

Then, when the employee arrives, you review the pre-frame to set the conversation up for success: "I know you told me that you want to get promoted to manager next year. There's a lot I've seen you do right, and overall, you're on track. However. There's one habit that's holding you back and I can help you change it. It will help your professionalism and you'll need it to show you're ready for the management role. Can we talk about that now?"

See how that leads into a productive meeting?

A great pre-frame sets the goal for a difficult conversation as something positive to help the other person. If possible, refer to the pre-frame when setting the meeting, then verbally review it when starting the meeting and make sure the other person is in line with it.

Notice I ended the example with the question, "Can we talk about that now?" You can also ask "Does that make sense?" or another question they can answer with a "yes" as that allows them to give their buy in.

If you feel there's any doubt or confusion on their end, pause and ask why. This is where awareness and intuition together are very powerful. It's important to start the meeting on the same page, and if you sense that's not the case, get curious and ask them about it so they get their concerns out on the table.

Once you get used to pre-frames, you'll use them all the time, whether it's with a single member of the team, your CEO, or even the whole company. Every meeting has a frame—if nothing else, it's the title and description of the meeting. I recommend you use them every time, and put some thought into them.

Step 2: Realign

If a meeting is ever getting off track, it's helpful to simply realign to the original goal of the meeting, which is the same as the pre-frame.

In the scenario of someone arriving late to work or meetings, if they start to give excuses or get defensive, you would say something like, "Hey, I'm just here to let you know what you need to do to become a manager. After all, how can you be the leader when you're not fulfilling your commitments to your team?" Then, they will most likely calm down and listen again.

Then the next time you're in a meeting and it's getting off course, and you reorient it back to the original frame, you'll be showing your strategic leadership. People will notice you keeping the original purpose of the meeting in mind, and putting things back on track. That's powerful.

Step 3: Reframe

Viktor Frankl was an astonishing and unique person. He was an Austrian neurologist and psychiatrist in the 1940s. He was also Jewish. This landed him in three Nazi concentration camps during World War II.

It's estimated that in Auschwitz, one of the camps he was a prisoner in, the Nazis mass executed 800,000 to 1,500,000 people using gas chambers and other means. What makes his story so remarkable is that Frankl told himself that if he had to go through this tragic experience, he would do his best to learn from it and take away something positive for humankind.

He ended up surviving and his subsequent book, *Man's Search for Meaning*, was selected by the US Library of Congress as one of the top ten most influential books ever written. After most everything was taken away from him and the other prisoners, he realized that the only thing you can't take away from someone is the ability to make a choice. The freedom to choose.

"Everything can be taken from a man but one thing: the last of the human freedoms—to choose one's attitude in any given set of circumstances, to choose one's own way." - Man's Search for Meaning, Frankl, V., Beacon Press, 2006.

Frankl didn't sit idly by while he was imprisoned. He learned about human nature. He found that the prisoners who survived were the ones who had purpose. The ones who lost purpose died. He worked on his ability to choose. In one of the largest human rights tragedies the world has ever seen, he found beauty. Whether it was in the smallest amount of generosity from the guards or a family giving their last scrap of bread to an orphaned girl, he found and celebrated humanity.

It would have been easy for Frankl to think of himself as a victim, but he didn't. He declared he would use the experience to benefit humanity. That's called reframing.

Reframing is when you look at a situation differently—through a new frame. Leaders are experts at reframing, but you can use reframing anytime with anyone.

Here are a couple of examples of reframing:

- Is your industry headed towards a downturn? A reframe could be, "Great, it will weed out the competition, and maybe lead to some new acquisitions."
- Are you going through a divorce? The reframe: "Okay, that means you've been in an unhealthy relationship, and soon you'll free up energy and space in your life and find your true love."
- Have you lost a key employee? How this can be reframed: "Super, now's my chance to upgrade the position and bring in new energy."

If Viktor Frankl can do what he did in a concentration camp, surely you can do the same in the office. It does take practice to identify and reframe an issue but the more you do it, the easier it becomes. Remember what we learned in the beginning of the book about neuroplasticity? Neurons that fire together, wire together, so practice reframing and soon your brain will be wired to handle difficult conversations like a pro.

Back to our example with the chronically late employee. So far, you've pre-framed the meeting and realigned when necessary in the meeting itself. Now, if the employee is worried that they've lost the respect of their co-workers, help them reframe it. Explain how they are respected already, and when they show that they are willing to take ownership and make changes, they will earn that much more respect; the level of respect that it takes to be a leader.

If you've read this far, you know that keeping people's confidence and self-esteem high increases loyalty, engagement, and resilience—and creates leaders you can delegate to. Reframing is a huge part of that.

Step 4: Recap

At the beginning of the meeting—and before the meeting—you pre-framed the agenda. Throughout the meeting, when things got off track, you re-aligned and re-framed. You've made great progress and reached a resolution.

Now, at the end of the meeting, the final step is to recap the original pre-frame. It sounds something like this:

"At the beginning of this meeting we agreed that we would talk about ways you could become more professional, and position yourself for a promotion next year. Did we accomplish that?" If you've done your job, the answer should be a simple "Yes." Again, if they hesitate, or answer anything but "Yes," pause and talk to them about it.

Psychologically, this puts a positive and final conclusion on the meeting and highlights that the primary goal was accomplished. You'll notice that again I asked them to affirm with a "Yes." This is a good way to make sure that they're in agreement with your statement; just don't overuse it.

Utilizing these four simple steps in any conversation or meeting will enhance your effectiveness exponentially.

Exploration

Visualize a future meeting. Mentally practice or write down a pre-frame and recap, then think of a few realigns and reframes that you think might come up.

The Growth Leadership Path

Phase 4:
Strategy and Influence

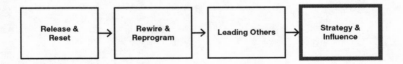

Now that you've cleared out your subconscious blocks, rebuilt your mindset, and are on the way to creating a high-performing team, what is your role? That's a key question leaders face as they evolve, and is the focus of the last phase on the Growth Leadership Path.

Earlier in the book, I mentioned a business owner named Tim. As we worked together, he put in place middle managers, and his time and energy were getting freed up. But what should he be doing now—where should he be investing this newfound time?

Because most people spend their lives being tactical and doing things, there comes a moment when they need to choose to "become strategic." This isn't about having a strategy, it's about adjusting your thinking and habits to support being strategic: being able to participate in and lead strategic meetings, learning how to build relationships with high-level people and have them hold you in high regard.

Through this mindset shift, you'll reach your full potential as a leader and transform into a strategic leader yourself.

CHAPTER 30:

Executive Presence

Have you ever been around someone who simply *carries* themselves like a leader? They have charisma and inner confidence, and radiate power, often without even saying a word. People are effortlessly drawn to them, like moths to a flame.

I work with a lot of leaders who have finally made it to the boardroom, or have a company large enough to have an executive team, yet they tell me, "People don't see me as the leader." Individuals like this may be liked and even respected, but they're missing that special something high-level leaders need to stand out and flourish. That special something is executive presence.

Executive presence is undeniable; you've probably experienced it yourself. People describe being able to feel a sense of power when this kind of leader is in the room; they have confidence and self-esteem, and they naturally command respect.

If you're looking to build your own executive presence, here are the ingredients:

- Operate from a strong sense of your authentic self—versus being driven by your ego.
- Lead with empathy coupled with emotional intelligence— as opposed to being top-down or transactional with people.

- Live a bold, fearless, positive life—by overcoming your own self-limiting beliefs.
- Be clear about your purpose and values and make decisions from that place—stop operating outside of your true self.
- Get to know and trust yourself; i.e. develop your own confidence and self-esteem.

We've covered each of these items in previous chapters, but executive presence is the accumulation of all of them together in one person, translating into who the leader is. Humans are energetic beings and our intuition can answer the question *"Who is this person?"* more than words ever can.

In fact, have you ever asked yourself that simple yet powerful question?

Who am I?

I'm not talking about where you were born, the degree you earned at school, or what your job title is. I mean who you are as a person. Again, think back to other leaders you've been around. How would you describe them? When you saw them, what feelings did they bring up in you?

Exploration

Take a blank piece of paper and spend some time with the question "Who am I?"

Get rid of all the "roles" like parent/programmer/sister/uncle, and write down your core traits. Who are you in any given situation?

To do this one right, you need to spend at least 30 minutes on it in two separate sessions.

When I work with people one-on-one, there's an extended version of this exercise that we spend three months on. The result is a powerful declaration of who they are, and this powers them forward with courage and confidence.

In each chapter of this book, we've taken who you are, released whatever isn't serving you, and kept and enhanced the parts of you that you want to keep. As you integrate and implement these pieces, the result *will* be someone who others naturally look to for leadership.

CHAPTER 31:

Becoming Strategic

The majority of leaders who come to me for help say, "I need to be more strategic." But strategic leaders don't appear out of nowhere. Usually, they come from a role as a tactical expert. Maybe they were a great programmer, a superstar marketer, or a successful salesperson—they're good at a "thing." As they start moving up the corporate ladder or scaling their business, they inevitably find themselves managing other people. From there, their actions need to be more strategic.

Unfortunately, they're quickly overwhelmed with daily tasks and can't get to their longer-term projects. *I know I need to delegate, I just don't know how!*

Or, they feel that when they try to say something in higher-level meetings, they either ramble on or don't make their point, and people don't respect them as leaders. *When I speak in our management meetings, I think people's eyes just glaze over and I lose them. Even worse, I think someone rolled their eyes when I was speaking!*

Sometimes, other people just don't see them as a take-charge leader. *My boss keeps telling me we need to be more strategic. I just don't know what that means?* Or *I know my team likes me, but they just don't respect me as a leader.*

In all of these scenarios, these former tactical experts don't know how to shift their mindset and it becomes an increasingly significant problem.

Becoming strategic doesn't necessarily mean developing a corporate or divisional strategy. It means thinking several months or years ahead in every decision you make. It means allocating part of your time to developing strategic initiatives. It also means being able to have high-level, big-picture discussions with CEOs and other executives so they see you as a peer.

The problem is that many of the skills you gained in order to succeed tactically actually go against what's needed to be strategic. "What got you here won't get you there," as coaching pioneer Marshall Goldsmith says. This means you have to learn a whole new mindset—but you also have to unlearn what made you successful in the first place.

When you were in your tactical role and something came up—a big, complex project, a problem with a big client, or a new initiative—you would jump all over it. You'd devote your focus, effort and skill to it, and at the end of the day turn a challenging situation into a big win. You looked like a superstar, felt great, and got praise from everyone around you.

Now, when something comes up, it's not your job to do it. You probably still do jump in more than you should because you like that feeling of accomplishment, showing people you're still valuable. However, every time you do that, it sets your team back. By jumping in, you're actually sending the message that you don't trust them, you aren't willing to teach and mentor them, and that it's all about you. Not what you want as an effective leader.

That's why the next addition to your leadership toolkit is delegation, which will free up time and energy to utilize in more strategic activities.

Exploration

Reflect on your current role to see opportunities to become more strategic:

- Are you spending too much time on tactical issues and need to delegate
- Does your team see you as a strategic leader?
- Do other high-level leaders respect you as a strategic player?
- Do you struggle to come up with strategies of your own?
- Are you active and effective in strategic meetings?

CHAPTER 32:

Successful Delegating

"I know I should delegate more, but…"

That's something I hear over and over from leaders at all levels. Everyone knows delegation is a must if growth is a priority, though many people have a resistance to letting tasks and responsibilities go. You need to delegate so you can become more strategic, move out of overwhelm, and leverage your efforts. And if you don't master delegation, you won't be able to achieve your full potential. Now that you have some psychology and neuroscience under your belt, let's go through some common delegation myths. As we go along, notice which ones apply to you:

Myth 1: This task is so small it's not worth delegating—it only takes a few minutes.

There are two problems with this. First, when growth is your goal, you should be making it your goal to get every single task off your to-do list that doesn't need to be there. That's the mindset that will free you up to lead. Second, every so often the "small" task doesn't go as planned and it soaks up time and effort to fix. That's time wasted that you haven't budgeted for—and is worth delegating.

In my smallest software company, one that wasn't large or complex enough to have full time accountants, we had gone through a few bookkeepers who never seemed to work out. All that needed to be done was the month-end process (above and beyond that, the CPA did all the heavy lifting). At the beginning of each month, we needed to categorize a few transactions in QuickBooks, then download and copy/paste them into the Excel spreadsheet which generated our P&L and KPIs.

Sounds pretty simple, right? It was. And it took only 15 minutes each month, so I started doing it myself. Everything was fine except: every few months something happened out of the ordinary. Sometimes we added an account and I had to modify the spreadsheet. Another time, we changed payment processors. Yet another time there was a problem with payroll. Each of these took a few hours of my time and because they weren't offloaded appropriately to begin, it became an even bigger issue. Don't fall into the same trap I did —nothing is too small to be delegated.

Myth 2: No one can do the task but me.

I'm sure you're very smart. You probably came up with many of the processes you're thinking of delegating in the first place. And you've been doing these things for years. But don't let your ego fool you into thinking you're *that* unique. You're smart, but you're not the only person on the planet who can handle it.

If a task is that complex that it can't easily be delegated, or no one truly can do it but you, it is a business risk. As a leader you need to come up with a better system that doesn't have a single point of failure—you.

Myth 3: I've tried to delegate task X before, but it got messed up.

In this scenario, the problem isn't that you delegated, it's *how* you delegated.

People have been delegating since the beginning of time, so it's not like you're somehow saddled with responsibilities that are more complex than people running multi-billion conglomerates. They've delegated successfully. You can too.

Delegation is so important that I'll share a bulletproof process that you can count on to handle it successfully later in this chapter.

Myth 4: I know I need to delegate, but I'm so busy that I can never find the time.

I hope by saying that out loud you realize how self-defeating and self-sabotaging that is. You're never going to get less busy—the busier you are, the more you need to start delegating right away.

This is one of the many times in leadership where you need to create extra time upfront so that you save time on the back end. In the next phase you'll learn a few habits to bring more strategic time into your life.

Myth 5: I would delegate, but I feel guilty. Some of the tasks are boring, repetitive, or not very fun, and I feel bad giving them to someone else.

First, it's great that you're being honest. Second, get started delegating right away.

As a leader you need to be handling strategic issues. Other people's jobs are to support you. If you're running around checking off to-dos that you can offload, you're actively holding the team back. Besides, most team members I know *want* to support their leader.

Myth 6: My people are already too busy.

Most likely they are busy, but your time is more valuable than theirs. That's not elitist, it's because when you aren't using your time for the things only you can do, your team will not be able to flourish. If you aren't flourishing, then the team isn't flourishing.

Your headspace and focus need to be on growing and optimizing the whole team and you can't do that for them if you don't let go of the tactical work. This is an extension of the **Pyramid of Values**—your value is being the conductor, not playing the instrument. Know your position and play it.

Myth 7: They don't know how to do it.

True, there are things your team doesn't know, but teaching them is called mentoring and is part of your responsibility as a leader.

You need to upskill your team and give them more responsibility. If you don't, they'll get bored, stale, and complacent—and either leave, or even worse, stay.

The delegation process is an ideal way to form closer bonds with your team as you coach them and show that you trust them as you expand their responsibility and skillset.

Myth 8: If I delegate, my role is at risk.

Fear is real, especially to the ego, so I get that some people may be threatened by delegating. But I've never seen a manager get fired because they were no longer valuable due to delegating. If you were to get fired, or made redundant, it would be for another reason—your salary is too high or your boss no longer sees your value.

Delegation is a strategic behavior that shows you're thinking about resource usage, the bigger picture for the business, and optimizing your own performance. If you don't want to be considered strategic, don't delegate.

Why People Don't Delegate

When you get right down to it, most of the time, guess what's to blame for the fact that you don't delegate? If you said your ego, you're right. Small, repeatable tasks you do every week or month give you a small dopamine hit when you get them done. They are quick, easy wins for your ego—something that's satisfying without any challenge or risk.

Plus, the ego likes that control factor, which is anti-delegation. That's why the ego will work subconsciously to hold onto tasks. That's why it's been so challenging for you to let them go.

When leaders come to me and say, "I'm overwhelmed and don't know where to start," I open up their calendar and task list and go through it with them. Within 15 minutes, we've cut their number of to-dos by half and taken hours of non-necessary meetings off of their upcoming schedule. Don't get caught up in the addiction of being busy and doing tasks.

The Delegation Transition Process

Here's an easy-to-follow system I call the Delegation Transition Process. It's designed to give peace of mind to both you and the person you're delegating to (let's call them the delegatee).

Start by picking the task or process you want to delegate. Complex tasks should have a planned, gradual turn-over. In a planning meeting before the delegation happens, figure out which one of you is doing which task, and define milestones for when the delegatee will take over responsibility—be explicit about that during the whole process.

You might say: "I want you to be responsible for this task, project or result by the end of the month. Until then, we'll work on it together so you can learn the ropes." You don't want confusion around who owns what process by when.

Once you've picked a task and a timeframe for the hand-off, follow this step-by-step process:

Step 1: Shadow

Do the task or process yourself as you would usually would, but have the delegatee shadow you as you do. This just means having them follow along at each step. If part of the process is electronic, don't skip that. Copy them on that communication so they can virtually shadow you.

This step can be done once or many times depending on the complexity of the process, their capabilities, your ability to coach, etc. Don't assume they've learned everything the first time through.

Step 2: Document

Have the delegatee document the steps either during the shadowing or afterwards—this becomes part of your standard procedures manual. Review the procedures written by the delegatee. Correct or add and discuss as needed.

The delegatee will learn the process faster and more deeply by writing it down, and you'll get a chance to review how well they've understood it.

Step 3: Reverse Shadow

When the delegatee feels comfortable, they then perform the process with you shadowing them. Make sure you give them the time and space to go through it on their own as much as possible.

While observing them, keep in mind they may do the steps in a different way while still getting the step done. If you see them veering off your way of doing things, ask them why with an open mind. Maybe it's an improvement.

Step 4: Support and Feedback

Once you have some confidence that the delegatee can do the task, stop shadowing them and move into a supporting role. What's important is to have check-ins after they take the task from you. These are necessary because when someone takes over a task, they often don't want to ask questions so that they seem smart.

The first few times the delegatee does the task on their own, have a mandatory call afterwards. It could be just two to five minutes long if it's a simple task. Ask them how it went. Try a few probing questions so you get a sense for how they did. Audit the task so *you* have confidence that they know what they're doing.

The two keys to this process are (1) to develop a gradual transition so everyone feels comfortable and has a chance to ask questions, and (2) to have follow-up meetings and reviews to give the delegatee support. Your experience and extra set of eyes will make sure the hand-off is a success.

Now that you have a proven process for delegation, there are no more excuses. What's first on your list to get off your plate?

Exploration

Write a list of all your responsibilities. Note down which ones you absolutely can't offload and why. Wait a day then review the list again. Make sure your reasons are still valid.

Make an action plan to delegate the tasks that aren't critical for you yourself to do.

CHAPTER 33:

Thinking Strategically

Thinking strategically is a creative process, and in order to be creative you need space and the proper environment. This means dedicated time for strategic thinking. As one example, I know a strategic advisor named Warren Rustead who, at this stage in his career, is a board member to a slew of companies. He is gifted at strategic thinking, and every day he spends four hours in his office alone, without distractions, intentionally focused on it.

People aren't born strategic thinkers; it's a learned skill. I read once that when Google was scaling quickly, it made time to have "yearly" strategy days...*once a month*. And Bill Gates famously goes away twice a year to disconnect from all technology. He calls them "think weeks."

To help us see where your strategic work is, let's borrow from a model you may be familiar with and adapt it to strategic thinking. The Time Management Matrix from Stephen Covey (Figure 22: The Time Management Matrix) categorizes tasks into four quadrants. On the top of the chart are urgent and non-urgent tasks. On the side are important and non-important tasks.

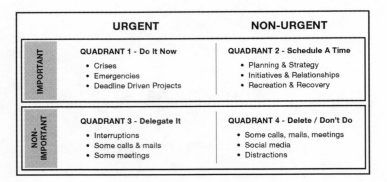

Figure 22: The Time Management Matrix

In Quadrant 1, we have Urgent and Important tasks. Examples of this kind of task include responding to customer issues, fire-fighting, production crises, etc. As a leader, you should always be working to delegate as many of these as you can.

In Quadrant 3—we'll come back to Quadrant 2 shortly—we have Urgent and Non-Important tasks. Here we have necessary, functional work such as reporting, administration, public relations such as interviews or press, etc. And yes, if you thought to yourself *I should be delegating these*, you're 100% right.

Next in Quadrant 4, we have Non-Urgent and Non-Important tasks, things like social media, fantasy football teams, gossip, over-analysis and perfectionism. These should be flat out avoided unless they provide stress relief and fun; just be honest with yourself about that and make sure you limit them.

Finally, we come to Quadrant 2, tasks that are Non-Urgent and yet Important. This category is where creative work lives. Here we find future planning, strategic partnerships, and even proactive recruiting. This is where the gold is and where time should be spent thinking strategically.

If you have question marks about what it means to think strategically, look for the activities that belong in Quadrant 2 and focus there. Most leaders are so addicted to spending time on the Urgent parts of the matrix that the Non-Urgent—yet strategic—quadrant gets forgotten.

The Power Hour

A very practical way to create structure to support your strategic thinking is something called the Power Hour. How often you do this is up to you, although anyone in a leadership or management role should consider once a week the minimum. Here I'll lay out the ideal scenario for a Power Hour; as with any other tool, make sure to adapt it to suit you.

Step 1: Block the first hour in your day.

This means the first part of your work morning—it's best after you're ready for work, but before you've opened your laptop or checked your email. (If you check your email first thing in the morning, stop it! Give your brain the morning to rest.)

Block out this hour in your calendar so you know that no one is expecting you. Even better, block out the first 90 minutes, so you can get caught up after the hour.

Step 2: Take a 15-minute walk.

Don't take your phone. Take a pen and paper if you like, to note down anything that comes to you. There's something about walking and being out in nature that helps your mind process what it needs to.

You might choose a theme to think about: a relationship you want to fix, a new partnership you want to develop, expansion into a new geography, etc. It can be any initiative, problem, or something you want to improve, now or in the future, and Something that's needed to grow your team, business or career long-term.

Maybe it's getting a head start on a big proposal, writing a job description for a new hire, or outlining a new referral program. It could be paging through your LinkedIn connections and dropping a note to some old contacts to see what they've been up to. Or Googling a few of your competitors.

Or, on some days, just go out with no agenda and let your mind wander.

If you think this sounds like a waste of time, then you need it more than anyone. Giving your brain unstructured time to go where it wants to go is a necessity, especially in today's over-scheduled world.

Step 3: Work on something strategic.

The result of your walk will be that you get more clarity about something strategic. Either a new strategic task will pop into your mind, or you'll creatively play with an existing initiative, and by the time you return from your stroll, you'll have new insight and a desire to execute on it. Then when you get back to your desk and computer, get right to work on it.

That's it. Just three simple steps. Once the Power Hour is over, you can go back to your day knowing you've got a strategic head start to the day and worked on something important for long-term growth. As this becomes a habit, your brain will naturally be wired to think this way, and it becomes part of your mindset. That's when thinking strategically becomes second nature.

Strategy Hacks

Here are a few other techniques to develop your strategic thinking:

A fun exercise I used to run with my executive team once a month was to go to a hotel restaurant for a strategic lunch. There, we would talk about what we could do, or where we could go as a company—but it had to be at least a year or more in the future.

At most of these strategic lunch meetings, especially at first, the team would start by trying to solve tactical problems. I had to coach the team to expand their thinking. We would play with different strategies and growth opportunities, discuss where the industry was headed and how we could take advantage of that. It was a fun, light meeting because it was all just speculation. No one committed to anything.

This format was great because my team didn't spend nearly as much time thinking strategically as I did, so this got them into the habit. As a result, the whole executive team started to think more boldly about the potential for our business.

One final strategy hack is to spend 30 minutes a week reviewing strategic news sources. This could be thought leadership articles on industry websites where you keep abreast of the latest trends, terminology, and technologies.

Exploration

Right now, schedule two Power Hours in your calendar. Try to get them in first thing in the morning.

Have a conversation with your team or a peer on what the future may look like in a year or more.

Spend a few minutes looking at strategic news in your area, or just in general. Then take a few minutes to digest what you've read and look for ways it applies to you.

Once you implement a few new strategic thinking habits, you'll start coming up with other ways to nurture big-picture ideas. That's what happens when your mindset switches from tactical to strategic.

CHAPTER 34:

Strategic Decision Making

Tactical managers have a habit of making decisions that are focused on solving the immediate issue. Thinking strategically—and that covers decision making—takes into account the medium and long term as well.

Think of any decision as having three timeframes associated with it:

- The immediate, or short-term timeframe, which solves the immediate problem.
- The medium timeframe, which ensures the solution integrates with other areas of the business and culture.
- The long-term timeframe, which makes sure the course of action is aligned with the overarching strategy of the business.

For example, let's imagine you're the manager of a marketing team with an innovative culture. Your team is doing well working with other departments in the company. You also know that the long-term strategy of the company is to expand into the Middle East.

You just lost a key digital marketing expert, and that empty position is creating a great deal of stress. Using a tactical approach, the priority would be to find someone with the right skillset as soon as possible and bring them on board—this would immediately resolve the pressure on you and your team.

However, a better, medium timeframe way to fill this role would be to let the process unfold without rushing. Find someone who will gel with, or even enhance, the special culture of your team. This may mean a delay, but you'll save headaches later.

Even better than that, you can use a long-term, strategic timeframe, and look for someone with the skillset you need, who's a great fit for your culture *and is experienced within the Arabic and Middle Eastern market.* This hire would be a proactive, strategic choice.

Exploration

What are some of the decisions you've made over the past few days?

In each case, did you successfully consider the three timeframes: short, medium, and long? If not, what could you have done differently?

What are some of the decisions you have coming up? How can you address the short, medium and long-term timeframes for each one?

CHAPTER 35:

Relating Strategically

The last time you met with someone like a senior executive, a board member, or someone in private equity or venture capital, did you feel intimidated—like they wanted to have a strategic conversation and you couldn't meet them on that level?

It's quite common to feel this way. Just like strategic thinking, strategic relating is a skill you can develop, and there are a few ways to do that.

Strategic Mapping

Every individual has a unique set of drivers—things they're motivated by—rooted in their personality type and their role. A VP of Marketing has different goals and drivers from a Chief Operations Officer for example, even if they work in the same company. As we learned in the chapter on Leadership Types, Dominant Commanders, Visionary Influencers, Logical Creators, and Supportive Collaborators are each driven by very different things.

On your journey to reaching your full potential as a leader, there will be a quite a few different people you need to relate to and connect with strategically. It can be helpful to create what I call a Strategic Relationship Map for each person. For example, if you're an IT director, you may have a Strategic Relationship Map to fill out for the CTO, who you report to; the COO, whose team you work with often; and the CEO, who your CTO reports to. These are key relationships you want to add value to, and relating strategically is the way to do that.

Or if you're new to a board or management team, fill out a Strategic Relationship Map for each board member.

Here are the questions that make up the Strategic Relationship Map:

- What is their role and what are their key activities?
- What are their objectives, targets and/or goals?
- How do these fit in with the company's strategy?
- Who do they report to?
- How do they get compensated and evaluated?
- What is their yearly strategy and key initiatives?
- What do they see as risks and obstacles?
- What are their risks and fears in their job?
- What were their past roles & why did they get promoted?
- What Leadership Type are they?
- What drives them?
  - When have I seen them happy?
  - Who do they gravitate towards?
- What upsets them?
  - When have I seen them angry?
  - Who do they dislike and why?

You don't have to answer all the questions for every single person, but you'll add to your ability to relate to them the more you do.

Some people wonder how they can answer these questions if they're not around the person very often. If you have mentors or contacts in other areas of the company, they may be able to help.

Another good tactic is to simply ask the person directly. If I was an executive and someone came up to me and said, "We don't know each other that well yet. What I do affects you and your department. Would you mind spending 30 minutes so we can get to know each other better, and I can find out what's important to you so I can make sure I'm delivering that?" I would be both happy and impressed.

When going about gathering this information, be careful that you don't come off looking like you're scheming or going behind other people's backs. Be open and authentic, ask questions out of genuine curiosity, and share about yourself.

Take note of the language that people use. You may call something a "budget" but they call it a "plan." Then you realize the rest of the board uses the term "plan"—so you start using that terminology as well. This may seem like a small detail, but it helps you see the world through the other person's eyes. This results in them feeling more comfortable around you, and subconsciously trusting you more.

Exploration

Think of the one person that has the most to do with your current and future success. Create a Strategic Relationship Map for them.

Strategic Conversations

As you're probably discovering, the higher up in an organization you are, the more responsibility you'll have, and the more you'll need to make decisions quickly based on limited information.

When leaders move into higher-level roles and talk to higher-ups, they often feel (or more accurately, their ego feels) that they have to prove themselves. This sometimes results in "diarrhea mouth"—taking a simple question and giving a long, detailed answer, until the eyes of the executive you're talking to start to glaze over.

When this happens, they're thinking one thing: *this person is not a strategic leader.*

If someone asks you a yes or no question, it's OK to answer with a "Yes" or "No." You can follow it up with a short qualifier if need be. For example:

"Can the prototype be ready within three weeks?"

"Yes, if I can borrow two engineers from quality assurance."

If they want more information they'll ask.

It's also OK to pause when you're asked a question to gather your thoughts; it's much better than running at the mouth. What's also useful is taking time to predict questions you might be asked and preparing short, strong answers in advance. Even if the exact questions don't come up, you'll be more confident and comfortable in meetings. I often do this before important meetings. It results in me being more confident and I get my points across much better.

You can prepare questions of your own as well, so you can take the driver's seat asking questions of others.

When you're promoted to a board or executive team, make a plan to get to know everyone one-on-one—ideally in a setting where you can fill in the questions on the Strategic Relationship Map you have of them. For example, you could invite them to coffee where you can find out about their personal drivers. It's much less intimidating to be in a room of people you've met before, versus a bunch of strangers.

When you're relating on this level, keep strategy, initiative, risks, and investment costs in mind at all times. You'll need to know the overall strategy of the company or the division and what initiatives are important to the CEO. If she wants to expand internationally, bring what you say back to the impact on expanding internationally. In other words, be relevant to what drives the person in front of you.

The higher up an executive is, the more they'll be concerned about risk. What's the risk of a given project? How does it affect other divisions? What's the overall cost? Bear this in mind in your conversations.

Questions are the language of strategy. Here are some additional examples:

- What does success look like in this project?
- What questions are we trying to answer?
- Why might the project fail?
- What's the worst-case scenario?
- Is this in line with our overall strategy?
- What else does this affect?
- Does the time and money spent justify the gain?

Asking the right strategic question at the right time can earn you instant credibility and respect from every attendee.

Exploration

Prepare for your next higher-level meeting. Think of a few questions you might be asked and write out some answers for them. Practice giving the answers out loud.

Also, review the questions from the Strategic Relationship Map shortly before the meeting. Be observant, and ask one of the questions—or a variation of one—if the right moment arises.

Strategic Networking

I once worked with a leader who confessed, "I go to a lot of networking events but only hang out with people that I know. I never get anything out of them; it's a waste of time." What so many leaders don't understand is when you walk into a networking event, you should understand two things. First, the value you bring to others, and second, how to align yourself with the right people.

When it comes to getting noticed, promoted, or funded, it's all about strategic networking. Before you head to a networking event, identify who you want to talk to. Do research on LinkedIn and Twitter and see if you can find out anything about them. Consider sending them a message to let them know you'll both be at the function. Then when you see them there, striking up a conversation will be very natural.

Always make sure your confidence game is on point—you want to show up as powerful yet open. Remember that someone who's aggressive and loud is being driven by their ego. The person who introduces themselves, makes eye contact, and listens a little more than they talk is the confident one.

Ask open-ended questions when you meet somebody for the first time, especially someone at a higher level. Listen for a while. Most likely, after a few minutes, they will ask about you. Mention your successes and opportunities, and how those tie in with something they're interested in. Don't ever ask for a favor, like a referral or promotion, right away. You might talk about a relevant win you had, or something interesting or fun.

Here's another place preparation comes in. It's fairly easy to predict the questions you'll be asked at a networking event. Have a few answers ready that aren't just factual but fun and engaging that show off your personality. Talk about what you love doing, something funny that happened to you lately, or something else slightly off the normal path—the goal is to get an interesting two-way conversation going and have them remember you in a good light. You'll do that through an authentic connection, not by showing them how smart you are or your past accomplishments.

My last tip for strategic networking is to keeping things moving—know when the conversation is coming to a close and move on to the next person. Simply say, "Hey, it was great to meet you. I'm going to go network some more." Then exchange business cards or connect on LinkedIn. They'll be just as happy as you that you kept things moving, and you'll meet a whole lot more people that way.

If you work for a larger company and you're going to an internal networking event, identify those who can help your career ahead of time. Get a sense—through their blogs, posts, and mutual friends—of who they are and what they're about. Then do your best to find them at company functions or join internal groups they're part of. Introduce yourself and start a strategic conversation. I've seen this kind of legwork lead to multiple wins for people I know—in the form of promotions and funding.

Exploration

For an upcoming networking event, if you can, research some of the attendees. Pick a few you'd like to meet. Connect with them on social media and suggest you talk at the event.

Think about or write down a few interesting ways you can answer the question *"what do you do?"*

CHAPTER 36:

Solving Complex Issues

Can you remember the last big decision you had to make that took up significant mental energy, maybe even causing you to lie awake at night? Perhaps you're facing a challenging decision even as you read this. If so, you're probably like a lot of leaders whose minds race through the day playing out every scenario, leaving you tired and irritable.

When it comes to strategic and complex decision-making, below is a tool I've developed that can be used for anything that's eating up your energy. The outcome is clarity with less stress. What's unique about this tool is its focus on bringing you to a better emotional state and presenting information in a way that you can process.

Your brain races around because it's trying to categorize information. Once you lay out the information in a structured way, your brain can slow down and find rational ways to solve the problem.

I call this tool the Complex Decision Worksheet.

Get started with a couple pieces of paper or your notebook, along with your favorite writing instrument.

Step 1: Name It

The first thing to do is give this situation a name. When I lead people through this process, it's interesting to see how this step, a seemingly basic one, gives them pause. The name should be simple, to the point, and just a few words. It's OK to take a few minutes to think about what it will be. Once you've got it, put it in big block letters at the top, in the center of your page.

Examples:

Let's say you have an employee named Frank who's not engaged with his work, you're not sure why, and you don't know how to address it. It's giving you anxiety. Possible names for this situation could be: Getting Frank Engaged, Connecting With and Serving Frank, or Creating a Culture of Excellence. You can see how each of the names brings a slightly different emphasis.

Or, imagine you're trying to work out if you should acquire a company—let's call it XYZ Corporation—and because it's a big decision, your brain is spending a lot of energy on it. Some possible names: Evaluating the XYZ Opportunity, Potential to Expand our Product Portfolio, or Strategically Considering the XYZ Acquisition.

Step 2: Ideal Resolution

Next, consider your ideal resolution to the problem. What's the best-case, yet reasonable way this could turn out? Just as in the previous step, this may take some time to think through, so don't rush. Under the title, write down "Ideal Resolution:" followed by what you came up with.

Examples:

Ideal Resolution: Frank catches on and gets inspired and engaged very quickly. He becomes a high-performing employee with a great attitude.

Ideal Resolution: We acquire XYZ company for less than $1,000,000 and the acquisition and integration goes very smoothly.

Step 3: "T" — Fact or Fiction

Now make a "T" chart, dividing the page into two columns. In the top left, above the line, write "Fact," and in the top right, write "Fiction."

Fill in the chart by writing what you know to be absolute truths on the left, and on the right, what you're making up, or anything you don't know to be 100% true. This will show that you're worrying about a lot of things you don't actually know to be true. Absorb that reality as you look at your T chart. This can go a long way toward alleviating your stress.

Examples:

Fact	Fiction
• Two people have asked me if Frank is OK • Frank has fallen behind in deliverables	• Frank doesn't like working here • Frank doesn't like me

Fact	Fiction
• Someone told me XYZ are looking to be acquired • XYZ have a product that would fit our portfolio well	• They will want a lot of money for their company • It will be a long, drawn out process

Step 4: Worst Case Scenario & Alternative

Now, write down the thing you're really afraid will happen. You'll lose your job? End up homeless? With no friends? Be as honest as you can.

Ask yourself *if that were to actually happen, what would I do?* Then write down a short action plan. What you're doing here is reassuring your brain: even if the worst-case happens, you have a plan for it, and the world won't fall apart.

Examples:

Worst case scenario: Frank doesn't like it here anymore. He will quit.

Alternatives: I will hire someone better, someone who's engaged, and we'll be in a stronger position overall.

Worst case scenario: XYZ Corporation is going to have too high of an asking price, or they aren't in a position to sell, and we won't acquire them.

Alternatives: We'll just continue with our present growth strategy.

OPTIONAL #1:

In addition to the one you just wrote down, list as many alternative solutions as you can think of to "what would I do?" It's a great way to open up your thinking, and you'll feel reassured knowing you have many different routes you can pursue—if an alternative is even needed.

OPTIONAL #2:

You've learned a lot about psychology as you've read this book, so let's go deeper by taking one more step. In this situation—the one you named in step #1 above—ask yourself, *"What am I really scared of?"*

I did the steps in this exercise this morning for a complex problem that kept me up last night. It turns out that behind the anxiety was an old, irrational self-limiting belief.

Step 5: "T"—Control and Can't Control

Next on your Complex Decision Worksheet, create another "T" and at the top, write "Can Control" on the left, and "Can't Control" on the right.

Fill in the left column with the things you feel you can control. (Remember, you can only control yourself!) Then in the column on the right, write everything that's out of your control. (Everything except yourself.)

This will realign you with what's productive to focus on in the situation. Take a moment to assess what your answers mean to your decision.

Examples:

Can Control	Can't Control
• How & when I approach Frank	• Frank's reaction/ response
• How I can frame the conversation, how I can be curious and compassionate and in my authentic self	• If Frank is willing to change
• How I react & respond	• If Frank wants to quit

Can Control	Can't Control
• How & when I approach XYZ company • The offer I make them • My energy throughout the negotiations	• If they accept my offer • How quickly they respond in the negotiation process • How they behave during the negotiation process

OPTIONAL:

In a new section, list the lessons you're learning from going through this decision-making process. For example, if you're going through a lawsuit, you're almost definitely learning valuable lessons. Things like: how the legal system works, how contracts work, how to protect yourself in the future, and how to emotionally care for yourself when in a legal battle—all crucial wisdom for a high-level leader.

Step 6: Next Action

Finally, write the heading "Next Action:" and list the steps you'll take. Once you've completed the action, you can come back to the sheet, cross it out and write in the next action you'd take after that. By doing this, you've alerted your brain to the fact that you know what's next, and you're going to do it.

Or, if you can think of the next several actions, you can list them all and cross each one off as you go. Crossing actions off when complete is a great psychological hack as it gives you a sense of completion. Then you'll have momentum to take with you into your next to-do.

My last helpful hint with regards to the Complex Decision Worksheet is to *keep it with you*. That way if another piece of information pops into your head, you can write it down on the sheet. Your brain will pick up the fact that you've recorded this new piece of data and know that it's free to continue relaxing.

Exploration

Is there something weighing on your mind or a complex decision coming up? Do a Complex Decision Worksheet for it for more clarity and peace.

CHAPTER 37:

Diversity and Inclusion

Let's be clear: I am not a diversity and inclusion (D&I) expert and I debated with my editor about whether I should even include this chapter. I'm still learning how companies and leaders can create diverse, inclusive, safe, and empowering workplaces, and based on my research and experience, I feel I'm just scratching the surface. However, I believe it's too important of a subject to not include in a book about leadership.

The purpose of this short chapter is two things. First, to give you some context around why diversity and inclusion does not happen naturally so you're aware of that bias. And second, to pre-frame the importance of making a commitment to diversity and inclusion.

There have been a lot of studies on the business case[30] and the fairness case[31] to actively stand for diversity and inclusion in your businesses and teams—and if you aren't familiar with either of those cases, I encourage you to educate yourself. The reasons to take a

30   Dixon-Fyle, S., Dolan, K., Hunt, D. V., & Prince, S. (2020, May 19). Diversity wins: How inclusion matters. McKinsey & Company. https://www.mckinsey. com/featured-insights/diversity-and-inclusion/diversity-wins-how-inclusion-matters

31   Thoroughgood, C. (2020, May 19). Fairness or profits? how to frame diversity and inclusion initiatives. Villanova University. https://www.villanovahrd.com/single-post/2020/05/19/fairness-or-profits-how-to-frame-diversity-and-inclusion-initiatives

stand on this are more compelling than ever. For example, McKinsey's latest reports[32] show that financial performance increases by 25% to 36%. These are not small studies; the latest data was collected from more than 1,000 large companies around the globe.

With that said, you should know that your brain is wired *against* being diverse and inclusive so you have to be active and purposeful to overcome this. If you've ever been on a team where everyone looks and acts the same, it may have been fun at first. But performance was most likely lackluster, or definitely not as high-achieving as it could have been because groups that lack diversity:

- Are not as creative
- Do not foster different viewpoints
- Lack healthy tension
- Do not stress test their ideas as much because people tend to agree with each other too quickly.

From a neurological standpoint, we've covered the similarity-attraction effect in an earlier chapter. To recap, with similarity-attraction, humans have historically felt more comfortable, more validated, and more accepted by people who talk, look, and act like themselves. That's the exact opposite of what we need.

In the initial stages of understanding diversity and inclusion, keep in mind that your ego may be subconsciously drawn to having people around you who are like you. Reflect on this anytime you need to make a personnel decision. Do you have a subconscious bias? The answer is almost certainly yes. Now that you're aware of it, what does your authentic self say about what you want to change?

When I worked in Asia, I was keenly aware when I was the only white person in the room. I knew my mannerisms and customs

32   Dixon-Fyle, S., Dolan, K., Hunt, D. V., & Prince, S. (2020, May 19). Diversity wins: How inclusion matters. McKinsey & Company. https://www.mckinsey.com/featured-insights/diversity-and-inclusion/diversity-wins-how-inclusion-matters

were different and I was always on edge, at least a little bit. But that was an easy situation compared to many. I haven't lived a life having been historically oppressed or underrepresented. I was just temporarily in a different country, and I had my usual confidence from my life in the United States.

Imagine if you were the only woman, the only black person, or the only trans person in a board meeting. Or, imagine you were the only black trans woman in your industry. How would you feel? Keep that in mind when you bring in new people. Give them your full support and go the extra mile to collaborate with them and set them up for success.

Finally, be aware of your judgments. The world is changing fast, and that isn't going to stop anytime soon. In the last few years, we've seen the implementation of genderless restrooms, and requests from HR departments to have people specify their preferred pronouns—she/her, they/them and he/his, and others.

My thoughts are this. If I don't know enough about a topic, and I want to form an educated opinion on something, I should talk to the people who are directly affected. I've found that listening to first-hand experiences and real-life stories gives me the most valuable and accurate insights.

If you're white, middle or upper-class, and educated, take a moment to consider the exciting doors and opportunities that have automatically been there for us—even the path of leadership we've been exploring. I bring this up so we can all approach this topic with empathy. Remember that as a leader, the more you can be attuned to your team, the better you can support them.

Leaders are always growing themselves and their team while looking for ways to help humanity. Anytime you can help team members—whatever their background and whoever they are—and encourage them to express themselves authentically, everyone wins.

Exploration

Reflect on your current knowledge and beliefs about diversity and inclusion. Do you believe you are as educated as you should be around those subjects? Make a plan to get yourself up to speed.

Could you have some race or gender biases, either conscious or subconscious? Think about ways you can overcome these.

Reflect on your current situation and team in general. How diverse are they? What can you do to improve this?

Mentally go through your team one-by-one. Do you believe, as their leader, you're giving them enough support? Do some research, or get some help from an expert to create a safe, authentic space, and make time to connect.

CHAPTER 38:

Leading the Way
for Humanity

In 1776 Adam Smith wrote *The Wealth of Nations,* which is widely regarded as the first modern work of economics and the precursor to the free market and capitalism.

What many people don't know is that Smith, who taught at the University of Edinburgh and later the University of Glasgow, was also the head of the Moral Philosophy department. His precursor to *The Wealth of Nations* was *The Theory of Moral Sentiments,* in which he talked at length about how people are both driven by self-interest and the pleasure (or benefit) of others.

When you look closely at both works together, it turns out Adam Smith was founding a new approach to economics with the goal of having everyone thrive. He specifically mentions how the free-market divides resources equally while it advances the interests of society.

In short, over the course of time, as the world has moved from the communist, socialist, feudalist, totalitarian, monarchy and authoritarian systems to a market economy (capitalism), there have been fewer wars and life has substantially improved.

With that historical context, let's now look at the number of people living globally in "absolute poverty" since 1820 (Figure 23).

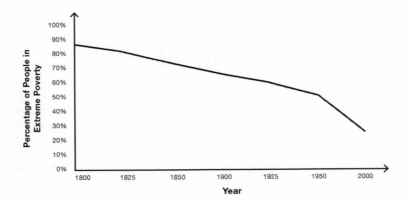

Figure 23: Extreme Poverty Over Time[33]

You can see from the graph that extreme poverty has dropped dramatically. Capitalism works. Using this one criteria, it works really well. Also, IT IS NOT PERFECT. And leaders who are willing to wield their influence can be part of the solution to make the system work even better.

When managers embrace Growth Leadership, and lead from their authentic self and a place of service, they are much more successful in the long run. From there, the market naturally helps them provide solutions to our systemic problems.

I experienced a turning point in the conversation about my business leading the way for humanity after I read the book *Firms of Endearment* by Raj Sisodia, who later went on to co-found Conscious Capitalism with John Mackey, the founder of Whole Foods. That book taught that conscious companies—firms that are truly

---

33   Roser, M. (2021, November 22). Extreme poverty: How far have we come, how far do we still have to go? Our World in Data. https://ourworldindata.org/extreme-poverty-in-brief

fueled by passion and purpose and come from a place of service—perform better over the long run than non-conscious companies.

In fact, conscious companies have outperformed the S&P 500 by 14 times over a period of 15 years.

The reason they perform so well is that their values line up. The values of the board or owner match the values of the CEO, which match the values of the executive team, which match the values of the leaders and managers, which match the values of the employees, that match the values of the customers, that also match the values of vendors, partners, and other stakeholders.

This creates an internal culture that is laser-focused on the purpose of the company, and it also creates unshakeable loyalty from customers because everyone through the value chain knows that the game being played is about more than money. Yet these are the companies that made the most money over the long term. This inspired me so much that I became President of the Board of Directors for my local Conscious Capitalism chapter.

If you read Jim Collins' seminal business book *Good to Great*, conscious companies even outperformed "Good to Great" companies by a factor of six. A "Firm of Endearment" has a purpose beyond making money; it has a values-based culture, and what Sisodia calls a SPICE (Society, Partners, Investors, Customers, and Employees) stakeholder approach to decision-making. All things that you as a leader can choose to learn from and create.

Because of the way the free market works, especially now that more and more leaders are evolving into Leadership Mindset 2.0, companies are leading the way to solve the issues the world is dealing with.

From steel created from hydrogen and non-fossil fuels (H2 Green Steel), to eliminating food waste (Goodr), to revolutionizing supply chains (Seurat, Sourcemap), business is on the forefront of creating innovative solutions to the climate crisis and sustainability.

Larger companies are listening to the experts, their customers, and their employees to make real changes as well. For example, Microsoft plans to shift to 100% renewable energy by 2025 and become carbon negative by 2030. By 2050, it hopes to remove all the carbon that the company has been responsible for since its founding in 1975[34].

Slowly but surely, companies are also developing programs to become more diverse, helping historically underrepresented groups of people, and giving back to the community more each year.

Johnson & Johnson, with over 132,000 worldwide employees, has a Global Diversity and Inclusion vision "to maximize the global power of diversity and inclusion, to drive superior business results and sustainable competitive advantage." To achieve this they have the Chief Diversity officer report directly to the CEO and Chairman. They've implemented employee resource groups, mentoring programs and a 'Diversity University.' And they've been named "Best of the Best" by *U.S. Veterans Magazine*; they're one of only two companies that have been on the *Working Mother* 100 Best Companies list for the past 28 years[35].

Almost every major company is now in a race to be a better corporate citizen, and with the transparency and interconnectedness of today's world, they can't fake it anymore. If you haven't heard

---

34   Noyes, L. (2022, September 26). The top 10 publicly traded companies Fighting Climate Change in 2023. LeafScore. https://www.leafscore.com/blog/top-10-publicly-traded-companies-fighting-climate-change-in-2021/

35   9 companies around the world embracing diversty in a big way. SocialTalent. https://www.socialtalent.com/blog/diversity-and-inclusion/9-companies-around-the-world-that-are-embracing-diversity

of it yet, ESG (Environmental, Social and Governance)—a set of standards measuring a business' impact—is a serious new focus of corporations around the world.

It's also not just companies who're seeing the change they can make—even wealthy entrepreneurs are giving away a majority of their fortunes and becoming philanthropists. Created by Warren Buffett, Melinda French Gates, and Bill Gates, the Giving Pledge is a commitment by 40 of America's wealthiest people to give away the majority of their wealth to address society's most pressing problems.

At the beginning of this book, I mentioned that the Growth Leadership Path is about growing both the business and the person. I find that as leaders progress on this journey and live from that authentic, service-based place, they naturally shift their energy to making the world a better place.

We—the world—needs you to keep evolving in that direction. Because you're a leader, people look up to you, whether you know it or not. And what you do, they will do. Our role models today need to be world-changers, and as a leader, you ARE a role model. Use everything you have—your voice, your position, your team, your company—to champion causes to move humanity forward.

You're meant for this. I believe in you.

Exploration

You've learned a lot up to this point. Now, viewing your role, team, and company as instruments to do good in the world, can you have even bigger, bolder goals and aspirations?

How can that bolder vision contribute to your company culture and even your relationships with customers and other stakeholders?

Now It's Your Turn

Leadership is one of the most challenging roles you will ever take on because it's never the same challenge twice; every day will ask something different from you, and what you need to do is keep learning and evolving. The pressure can be immense; everything falls on your shoulders, and when things go wrong, it will be your fault—but when things go well, the victory will go to the team or the company.

That's OK because that's part of what you signed up for as you accepted the leadership role. What's great is that the rewards are worth everything else you have to go through. Seeing your people step into their maturity and leadership as they succeed and grow, all due to you conducting the orchestra, is one of the most fulfilling feelings you can experience.

Look at all you've learned so far. You released your self-limiting beliefs and reset your mind. Then you rewired and reprogrammed yourself for natural confidence, self-esteem, and self-worth. You learned to lead others by understanding how people think and how you can give them purpose through serving. Then you learned how to shift into being a strategic, influential leader.

There's been a lot. Don't rush. Apply what you've learned here one thing at a time. Stay the course, and you'll get there.

To give you a head start and help keep things simple, I've picked three core concepts from the Growth Leadership Path for you to put into action. You'll be able to implement more tools in the weeks ahead, but if you only focus on these three for now, you'll make a lasting, significant difference right away.

1. Embrace your role as a leader

Your team wants you to lead them. Your company needs you to step up. Start thinking of yourself as a leader and own it—that means studying leadership, working on your mindset, and showing up stronger than ever for yourself and everyone else.

Always keep in mind the Foundational Truth of Leadership: that your leadership is a reflection of your relationship with yourself and commit to working on that. Be on the lookout for blind spots and self-limiting beliefs creeping in. Compassionately monitor your physical, mental, emotional, and even spiritual health. Make sure you're strong in your confidence and self-belief. You have a lot of influence over all of that.

Most of all, tell yourself, "I am the leader. And I can do this." Because you can.

2. Shift from your ego to your authentic self

Throughout the book, I've emphasized that our underlying focus is to become aware of your ego and work on shifting out of that into your authentic self. In fact, every tool you've learned here moves you from your ego to your authentic self in some way.

"Am I in my ego?" is the most simple and powerful question you can ask yourself at any given time for as long as you're leading others. Just by asking that question you'll become present, and most likely pop out of your ego. From there, see if you can move the needle even further, into your authentic self.

When you're interacting with someone else, you can apply this by asking, "Are they in their ego or authentic self?" If they're in their ego, ask the question "why?" Why do they need to protect themselves in this moment? Then adapt your approach to meet them where they're at. That simple act right there is an act of service.

3. Work the ARC Process

Commit to working the ARC (Awareness, Response, Compassion) Process, as it gives you a handy, multipurpose framework to use anytime.

Start with Awareness. Slow down. Ask yourself "What's really going on? What is the root cause of the issue I'm facing?"

After answering those questions, move to Response. "I'm probably *reacting*. What *response* can I choose instead?" Remember, responses are always from your authentic self. They come from a place of service, purpose, vision, values, and integrity. And since you paused in order to consider your response, you're giving your intuition the space to bring forward the proper tool to use next.

You'll answer questions such as "Do commitments need to be made, clarified, or renegotiated? Am I being judgmental? Do I need to move into acceptance? What's the next best action I can take now?"

Finally, move to Compassion. Are you judging yourself? How's your self-talk? Are you being hard on yourself or someone else? Give yourself a break and let it go. Remember that you're human. Forgive yourself and anyone else as needed and get back into that strong leadership mindset to keep doing an amazing job.

That's all you have to keep in mind in order to get started with your own Growth Leadership. Over time, you'll bring in additional tools until they become natural. You'll start to put more strategic thinking into your life, growing your influence. You'll trust yourself and your team more, raising your confidence and developing that strong executive presence. And you'll develop a loyal, engaged, high performing team with a strong culture.

If you enjoyed this book and want to shorten your learning curve as you and your team implement changes, go to www.RMichaelAnderson.com to explore my current programs and trainings.

Thank you for reading, and for your commitment to your leadership. I believe business leaders like you are the key to change all over the world. If I can ever be of service to you, please reach out.

Now it's your turn to fulfill your potential and become the powerful, compassionate leader that's there within you.

Lead On,
Michael
michael@RMichaelAnderson.com.

Afterword

It's been quite a journey writing this book. At the start of 2022 I was going through radiation treatment for cancer (all healed now and back to full strength!) and I needed a project I could dip in and out of depending on how I felt. After using and teaching these tools, skills and mindset shifts for over a decade, I knew that I wanted to put all of them into a book, and thus Leadership Mindset 2.0 was born.

I've worked on this book for over a year; it's been a labor of love, and I truly hope that it leads to more success, happiness, and love in your life. I'm here to serve, so if I can ever help you, or you just want to say hello, drop me a line at michael@RMichaelAnderson.com — I answer every email, I promise!

And since you've made it all the way here, I have a favor to ask you.

For authors like me, your book review can make a real difference. It lets other people know what you thought of it (after all, don't you read other people's reviews?) and that can be the difference between a potential new reader investing in this book or not.

Please take a few minutes and to leave a review. If you purchased the book on Amazon you can review the paperback book by going to: tiny.cc/reviewpaperback or by scanning the QR code below:

and if you purchased the Kindle / ebook, the review link is: <u>tiny.cc/</u> <u>reviewebook</u> or you can use the QR code below:

Also, remember to join my free communities to download templates, worksheets, trainings, and other resources that expand on the book. There's one on Facebook: <u>RMichaelAnderson.com/</u> <u>FBGroup</u>

and on LinkedIn: <u>RMichaelAnderson.com/LIGroup</u>

See you on the Growth Leadership Path.

Lead On,
R. Michael Anderson

About the Author

R. Michael Anderson, MBA, MA combines the real-life experience of founding, scaling and exiting three software companies with the educational background of a Master's Degree in Psychology and a passion for neuroscience. With this striking combination, he creates truly impactful transformation in leaders.

Stanford University brings him in to work with their start-up ecosystem, PwC has him work with their high growth CEO's, and companies like Microsoft, Salesforce, and Uber retain him to level-up their managers and executives.

With his background in psychology and neuroscience, he transforms managers and founders into true leaders with high-performing teams in high-growth companies. He's written two best-selling business leadership books, contributes to Entrepreneur.com, and is a former radio show host.

A former professional basketball player, the 6'8" Michael is hard to miss.

If you are interested in bulk-buying 10 or more copies of this book, or want to explore having Michael speak to, train, or coach your organization, send a message to info@RMichaelAnderson.com and a member of Michael's team will get right back to you.

Made in the USA
Middletown, DE
28 November 2023